More Praise for Stragile

"Giving context and a voice to applications in a rapidly changing world is what we do at CafeX. As outlined in Shawn's book, "Stragile", it is clear that the pace of innovation is increasing at a compounding rate, impacting how organizations will drive and adjust strategic execution and the results they yield. Platforms talking, seeing and even thinking are not science fiction; it is a reality that needs to be acted on. This book contains a unique set of stories, analogies and case studies on the potential impact innovation has for today's dynamic business."

—Dan Solito, COO CafeX

"ITSMA specializes in helping companies market and sell services and solutions more effectively. Our work comes down to Strategic Execution of programs that drive measurable results. Shawn has applied Account Based Marketing at several organizations. He has demonstrated an ability to adjust the strategic execution of those efforts to ensure measurable, reportable results to his customers and his organization. With entertaining and thought provoking examples, he outlines the profound impact technology holds when executing any strategy."

—Jeff Sands, Vice President of ITSMA

"CDC Software lets your telephony system talk to your applications and services. Stragile outlines the massive potential organizations hold by looking to apply technology to the art and the science of strategic execution."

—*Mathew Bieber, CEO CDC Software*

"Harvard Business School's Executive Education program, 'Aligning Strategy and Sales', is an immersive learning experience—one that empowers senior executives to reflect, recharge, and reemerge as visionary leaders. Shawn fully absorbed the program. The entertaining account of his experiences in Stragile illustrates both his perspective and his vision."

—*William Shea,*
Director, Corporate Relations and Market Development,
Harvard Business School Executive Education

STRAGILE

adjective: stra•gile \str'a- ˌjī(-ə)l\
To deftly identify and close gaps
between strategic plans and results
– Applying innovation and profiting
from the accelerating rate of change
in today's business

By

Shawn Jean

Stragile
Copyright © 2016 Shawn Jean

Printed in the United States of America
First Edition Printing

Design by
Arbor Services, Inc.
http://www.arborservices.co/

ISBN: 978-0-692-62063-2
LCCN: 2016900806

1. Title   2. Author   3. Business/Management

Contents

Preface

Consider these three numbers: 2,088, 21, and 72. What do these numbers mean? They are the 2,088 miles, 21 stages, and 72 seconds between the cyclists placing first and second in the 2015 Tour de France. They demonstrate how close the difference between winning and placing second can be over a long, grueling race. They show how the smallest change, understanding the implications of it, and reacting to it quickly can be the difference of seconds or minutes and winning or losing. They show the margin between winning and not winning is part technology (the bike and gear), part science (the training, planning, and nutrition) and part art (the athlete's "heart"). Now imagine a world where the average weight of a bike goes from ~15lbs (6.8 kg) to .00075lbs (.00034 Kg), resulting in less effort, less drag, and less road resistance that would have a colossal impact on the science and art of bike racing. This analogy is representative of the rate and type of innovation that can be applied to business and is a cornerstone of this book (this is real, is happening, and will be outlined in detail).

In business, the rate of change is happening at an increasing rate. As with the Tour De France, mistakes need to be corrected ever more quickly, and overall goals often need to be reexamined over short periods of time. Unless a company is agile and responsive, misalignment and "the gap" between strategy and results will grow, and the margin for error is smaller each day.

Assuming an organization has invested wisely in its executive leadership to set a strategy, I believe an organization will flourish when it can ensure alignment between strategy and results in a condensed time frame. There are proven methodologies, augmented by technology, that can drive this both efficiently and effectively. A key to success is gathering data and sharing it in a manner that cuts through the ego, emotion, and politics.

Over the last twenty years I have worked at one thing, understanding my organization and customers to determine how technology can help move the strategies and metrics their core valuation and business is based on. Over that time, I have seen many of these gaps and have some valuable information to identify them and close them.

I can recall my first experience and realization of the gap. I was an eager young executive working on a project that would change the way the company I was with would do business. It was at the "tip of the spear," with tens of thousands of man-hours and tens of millions of dollars invested in this effort. My job, at the time, was to determine the go-to-market model for this new offering and scale the sales of it via direct channel, system integrators, and service providers.

With a sense of excitement I attended meetings chaired by the CEO, enthralled by each exhilarating word of how this effort would not only change our company but the way our customers would conduct business. It was a logical offering; one could easily see how it could have an enormous impact in our space, and we had a jump on the market. Because I was well prepared, I had found the place where luck (preparation meets opportunity) would strike!

Or had I?

It soon became apparent that the teams on the organizational chart responsible for the strategic execution were neither aligned nor prepared to deliver. As the project came together, it became painfully clear we were not set to execute. As demand continued to grow, these groups became more determined to explain why the plan would not work and even countered the strategy; otherwise they would have to answer why they could not deliver and were not aligned to the stated strategy. While the market wanted the new solution on which we had hung our strategy, our organization was becoming more and more entrenched to *not* deliver it.

The project lingered on in this condition for many years but was never officially cut out of the scope of the organization. This project had been so pronounced and the leadership so outward on execution to the market that the result was both an internal and external credibility killer and widespread belief that the corporation couldn't execute on the vision. This had colossal impact on share value and employee commitment.

This condition is not unique. Such a dynamic can be the downfall of any particular entity.

At AT&T, I can recall my line managers and VPs scoffing at the idea that AT&T might be threatened by voice over Internet protocol (VoIP) as it became prolific and replaced our traditional voice service at a compounding and accelerated rate. The outward and inward clearly stated strategy from the company's CEO at the time, and his leadership, banked on this dynamic and were looking to replace the revenue with broader content over a network. But the company could not fathom a "non-per-minute" world and did not embrace the strategy. Therefore it was not executed successfully. The stock plummeted and the company was ultimately sold to SBC.

I've seen misalignment happen in real life, and I'm sure that you have too. I believe that too often in business, misalignment is the norm. This prevents a corporation rallying behind a strategy and executing to full life cycle. The technology now exists to enhance the art and science of executing a strategic plan and producing results aligned to that vison. I've written this book to show leaders and managers how to get into alignment, and even more importantly, how to stay in alignment even as conditions—both external and internal—change at a rapidly increasing rate.

The one thing that everyone in business can count on is change. *Stragile* can help you pivot from being a victim of change to profiting from it.

Introduction

If there's one thing we can all agree on, it's that the rate of change in the world is accelerating. The trends and fads of the moment vanish more quickly than they used to. What is cutting-edge today is quickly consigned to the dustbins of history. We look back on styles and customs that were popular ten or twenty years ago and they seem hopelessly quaint.

If you look at human history in context, it's a striking phenomenon. Take, for example, an average European peasant who lived from the year 950 CE to his death in 1010 CE. During his relatively long life of sixty years, it's possible that he witnessed *not one* technological advance. On the day that he died, his world may have been *exactly the same* as it had been on the day he had been born. From birth to death he used the same type of oxen to plow his fields, saw the same handwritten Bible in his local church, prepared his meals with the same iron pot over the fire, and wore the same clothing his father and grandfather had worn.

Yes, there were changes—our peasant may have seen slight advances in metallurgy, for example—but they came intermittently and took decades to seep into the fabric of society. The defining characteristic of his world was not one of change but of stasis.

Now add a thousand years to the birth and death dates of our peasant, and say that he lived an ordinary middle-class existence from 1950 to 2010. The changes that he experienced would be far too many to be enumerated here. But it's safe to say that unlike our medieval peasant, the person of the late twentieth century understood that the world is fundamentally one of change, not stasis. Change has become the norm, not the exception.

If our eleventh-century peasant were transported to our time, he would be astounded at how quickly the world changes and bewildered by the unrelenting flood of "newness."

The increasing rate of change can be measured. According to Kurzweil's law of accelerating returns, in the twenty-first century we won't experience a mere one hundred years of progress; by the yardstick we're accustomed to, it will be more like twenty thousand years of progress.

To put this into human perspective, this rate of change is analogous to the sprinter Hicham El Guerrouj, who's the current men's record holder for the mile, improving on his time of 3:48 to running the mile in less than two seconds! This dynamic will progress at a compounding rate to a point of "technological singularity" where machines can self-improve at a faster rate than people can improve them, reaching levels of intelligence and compressing innovation cycles beyond human comprehension.

This accelerating rate of change impacts every area of our existence, from our personal lives to how we operate our businesses. What year are you and your organization operating in? This book is about business strategy, and how the accelerating rate of change is a challenge not only on the obvious level of competitiveness in the marketplace but how strategic miscalculation and misalignment becomes more costly over time—and time is growing ever more compressed.

A year today isn't what it used to be in the twentieth century. It's gotten shorter, with more activity crammed into it.

The main reason strategies are not successful is they are not executed on or aligned to their goals. If an organization's stated strategy and goals do not align with what they do and the results they produce, then by definition they are rudderless.

This "gap" between strategy and results can have catastrophic consequences. Any delay in realigning strategy to goals will quickly become so pronounced that any strategies you have invested in may be rendered worthless. In today's fast-paced business world, your margin for error is shrinking. Even a small miscalculation—a tiny gap between operations and expected results—can quickly widen into an expensive chasm.

With persuasive explanations and fascinating case studies, this book combines these two dynamics and dramatically challenges the way we think of a strategy and the basic foundation and execution of it. While some things will remain more constant—I call them the "art" (leadership) and the "science" (basic human behavior and economic principals)— the technology changes cannot be underestimated and need to be factored into any organization's plans to be successful in today's world.

When we were kids, most of us played the game "telephone," where you formed a line of people and whispered a simple message to the first person. Then each person passed it on to their neighbor until the last person repeated what they heard. Here the original message was revealed, and invariably showed that the final message bore little to no resemblance to the original.

This is exactly what can happen in an old-fashioned vertically structured organization. When you add siloes that don't talk to each other, you have a recipe for disaster.

Now combine the concept of agile methodology with your strategy formulation and goal setting. Technology can play a critical role, such as putting information on a network of interactive monitors for everyone to see, and in which communication is both instant and two-way. With this one example we can see the impact that technology can have on strategic execution and identifying and removing gaps between the vision and reality.

This powerful and eye-opening book reveals the high cost of ignoring misalignment at any level and at any time—and points the way to the solution: getting *Stragile*.

The word "stragile" simply means a strategy that is agile. To be agile means to be proactive, aware, responsive, and willing to do what's necessary to meet the goals of the organization. It's an approach that unfolds over time and touches every aspect of your organization, from the front line to the boardroom. The ability to be stragile comes from a mastery of technology, science, and art, and having the insight to leverage them to achieve a perfect unity of purpose and results.

Through its use of revealing case studies, this book shows you how to prevent your project or organization from suffering miscalculations and gaps between real-life conditions and expected results. *Stragile* helps you to see those problems as they happen now, in real time, and quickly respond to close the gap and keep your organization on track.

Let's get started!

1. Misalignment Is Costly

On a cold Sunday night in April 1912, the biggest ocean liner in the world, the RMS *Titanic*, hit an iceberg off the coast of Newfoundland. Within three hours, the ship had gone to the bottom and over 1,500 people lost their lives. The great ship's maiden voyage had become a costly failure.

You may be wondering what this tragedy has to do with your business.

Hopefully, nothing. But it's very possible that your enterprise could suffer the same fate: you think you've got everything under control, you're steaming along at full speed—and suddenly you're facing disaster.

On that fateful night in 1912, something went terribly wrong. What was it? And what can you learn from it?

The problem was a serious misalignment of strategy and expected results, and you can learn plenty from it.

The obvious reason that the *Titanic* sank is because she struck an iceberg. But did the accident have to happen? Could the tragedy have been avoided and the passengers have landed safely in New York?

Of course it could have been avoided.

To find out how, let's start at the beginning, with the fundamentals.

The maiden voyage of the *Titanic* was not unlike any project or enterprise undertaken by any organization. It involved a huge financial investment, a tight timeline, defined goals, and in particular, the safety and well-being of over two thousand human beings.

During its lifetime, every project or enterprise goes through a series of well-defined stages. In the old days—the days of the *Titanic*—these stages were generally followed sequentially. They unfolded over time in a linear fashion, like a river flows over a waterfall. The stages included:

1. Set a desired result or goal.
2. Develop a strategy to reach that goal.
3. Make specific plans.
4. Implement the plans.
5. Get the results.
6. Evaluate the results.

In guiding your business or project, you would progress through each stage. At the end, you'd evaluate the results and then make any necessary changes.

In the case of the White Star Line, which owned and operated the *Titanic*, what were the stages they progressed through? They were these:

1. Set goal

The desired result was to profitably capture a significant portion of the transatlantic passenger business. Market leaders in this intensely competitive space included Norddeutscher Lloyd and the Hamburg Amerika Line (both German), Cunard Line and White Star Line (UK), Compagnie Generale Transatlantique (CGT) or French Line (France), the United States Lines (US), the Italian Line, and the Holland-America Line. All of these companies operated large, modern vessels that were only marginally smaller than *Titanic*, and many were either faster or more luxurious. To use an automobile metaphor, *Titanic* was not a Rolls-Royce; it was a really big Cadillac.

2. Create strategy

The goal would be achieved by building and operating a fleet of large, modern passenger liners capable of competing profitably at a premium level. Three of these vessels were the sister ships *Titanic*, *Olympic*, and *Britannic*. For the *Titanic*, a luxury vessel that was booked to capacity on her maiden voyage, the immediate return on investment was not a problem.

Fares charged on the *Titanic* were premium but not exorbitant. One-way fares for the transatlantic crossing (1912 currency) were £870 for a First Class parlor suite, £30 for a First Class berth, £12 for Second Class, and £3 to £8 for Third Class. Depending upon which currency converter you use, in today's dollars the price of the First Class parlor suite would be roughly $100,000, while the price of a Third Class ticket was about $600. Today, a one-way plane ticket from London to New York costs about $400 for economy up to $1,800 for first class. It's worthwhile to remember that today's flight takes about eight hours, as opposed to six days aboard the *Titanic*. Therefore a typical passenger jet that flies six days a week can generate six times the weekly revenue as *Titanic*.

It's also worth noting that in terms of long-term operational profitability, if the ship had carried more lifeboats—which were an *expense*—the ship would have been heavier and may have had less space for passengers, and hence a lower margin. Thus the decision to equip the ship with only the legally required number of lifeboats may have been based both on considerations of expense and of image—after all, it was unimaginable that dozens of lifeboats capable of carrying over two thousand people would ever be needed.

An important part of the business strategy pursued by the White Star Line was for the ship to make the Atlantic crossing *exactly on schedule*. The *Titanic* left Queenstown, Ireland, at two o'clock p.m. on Thursday, April 11. It was very important that the ship arrive at Pier 60 in New York exactly at dawn on the morning of Wednesday, April 17. While the ship's overall speed was important, sticking to the timetable was more important; arriving too early was deemed to be as unacceptable as arriving too late. When you've got John Jacob Astor on your ship, and he has instructed his chauffeur and his servants to meet the ship at Pier 60 at dawn on Wednesday, you'd better have your ship arrive exactly on time. It was a matter of prestige, or, as we would say it today, *branding*. The *Titanic* brand had to be the very best, because this would drive future sales. Among other things, being the best meant being precisely on schedule.

3. Make plans

What was the best way to ensure arrival in New York precisely at dawn on Wednesday?

To meet the schedule, the best way was to carefully chart the course and then stick to it. This included preplanning the ship's direction and speed over a period of six days.

One possible impediment to a smooth crossing was the presence of icebergs. In crossing the Atlantic, the *Titanic* planned a southerly route, where it was assumed there would be clear sailing with few icebergs. It was also assumed that in good weather, any iceberg in the ship's path would be clearly visible. Hence, in waters where icebergs were present, there was every reason to maintain the brisk rate of speed required by the timetable.

Therefore, in advance of the voyage this plan was approved: maintain a constant speed, steer south of icebergs, and if an iceberg were in the path of the ship, it could be easily spotted and avoided.

It sounds like a pretty good plan, and one that is similar to any business strategy. In a SWOT analysis (strengths, weaknesses, opportunities, threats) of the voyage, icebergs would have been recognized as a threat, but a minor one. A set of assumptions was adopted: we steer clear of icebergs, we don't slow down (which would throw us off schedule), and we assume that if the threat appears we can easily steer around it.

4. Implement plans

On the day and evening of the accident, numerous ships in the area reported icebergs. While other ships slowed down— and a few, such as the nearby *Californian*, even stopped—the *Titanic* did not alter its plan: maintain speed, maintain course. There was no recalibration and no reconsideration of either strategy or plans. As new and disturbing information came to Captain Edward Smith and the ship's owner, J. Bruce Ismay, who was on board, it was ignored. The ship's sailing plan was a good one and there was no reason to alter it.

At close to midnight, the threat materialized. A big iceberg lay directly in the path of the ship.

The lookout spotted the threat and sounded the alarm. The ship tried to turn. It was too late to avoid a collision. The iceberg ripped a gash in the hull, and the rest is history.

The case of the *Titanic* is all too common in business: set goal, determine overall strategy, make plan, execute plan, get results. If the results are disastrous, you just say, "Oh, we had terrible luck" or, "The competition was just too much" or, "We had bad timing."

What could the captain of the *Titanic* have done differently? In retrospect, it seems absurdly simple: when conditions change, it's time to circle back and realign the process. If necessary, change the strategy, change the plan, change the implementation, and even change the desired result. To her owner, it was unthinkable that the *Titanic* should arrive in New York at any time other than at dawn on Wednesday. If the ship had to slow down or change course, could the lost time have been made up during the two days following? Probably; the ship had never been operated at full speed. But this adjustment was never considered.

Aside from the tragic mistake of strategic inflexibility, the *Titanic* disaster revealed another common danger: the increasing rate of change. Your external business universe— opportunities and threats—is evolving quickly. Change is constant and can be dramatic.

The estimated elapsed time between when the *Titanic's* lookout spotted the iceberg and the ship's impact was about one minute.

Imagine what would be written in history if the iceberg had been seen a few seconds earlier?

Or if the *Titanic* had been able to turn more quickly? By contemporary shipbuilding standards, the *Titanic* was equipped with an obsolete rudder design. Rather than being agile—a word that we'll see often in this book—the *Titanic* was cumbersome. It was too slow to change course.

Here's one more thing to think about: the fact that circumstances can arise that are not part of your planned contingencies. When you make your plans, you may think you've considered everything that can go wrong in the future—but new circumstances may require a quick reassessment.

Here's an example. This may seem like an obscure detail of ship design, but it may have been critically important. The *Titanic* was equipped with three massive propellers—one in the center flanked by one on each side. Deep within the ship's engine room, a massive reciprocating steam engine powered the two outboard "wing" propellers, while the center propeller was powered by its own engine, a steam turbine that used recycled steam from the big reciprocating engine.

The important part of the story is that the two wing propellers could be operated in reverse, to make the ship back up or to slow it down. The center propeller could not be operated in reverse. It could only be thrown into neutral.

Normally, this would be a trivial distinction. A ship as massive as the *Titanic* would normally be operated in reverse only in port. The ship's designers and owners never imagined a scenario where on the high seas the ship would have to be suddenly and forcefully reversed. That sort of thing simply never happened—it would be like a huge semitrailer truck backing up in the middle of a highway.

When the iceberg was spotted, First Officer Murdoch, who was on the bridge, made the immediate decision to order the engines reversed and the rudder turned hard to port, or to the left.

Down in the engine room, the two wing props were thrown into reverse. The center propeller simply stopped turning, since it couldn't go into reverse.

Many experts have theorized that when the center propeller was shut off, the thrust of water over the ship's rudder—located directly in line with the center prop—was compromised. When the rudder was turned hard to port, it had less water to "grab" onto. The relatively small rudder was rendered even less effective than it could have been, and the ship turned more slowly than necessary.

Because of this idiosyncrasy in design, it may have been a better choice if Murdoch had ordered the ship to proceed at *full speed ahead* while turning hard to port. The ship would have turned much more quickly—perhaps quickly enough to miss the iceberg.

Sometimes in business it's necessary to put a full stop to a project that has fallen into misalignment. But sometimes it's better to *keep moving forward* while changes are being made. That's one of the keys to agility—being able to get into alignment while on the fly.

2. The Accelerating Rate of Change

In today's economy, change happens very quickly. A scenario that seems benign—such as encountering an iceberg in your path—can quickly become a disaster. Today, there is literally less time to correct problems than there was a hundred, fifty, or even five years ago.

The *rate of change* of our world—change driven by technology and human progress—is accelerating.

Moore's law reveals this perfectly. Named after Gordon E. Moore, the cofounder of Intel and Fairchild Semiconductor, it's the observation he made in 1965 that the number of transistors in a dense integrated circuit would double approximately every two years. Moore projected this rate of growth would continue for at least another decade.

His prediction proved accurate for several decades, and the law was used in the semiconductor industry to guide long-term planning and to set targets for research and development. But its effects are not confined to the semiconductor industry. In the late twentieth and early twenty-first centuries, digital information in all its forms has propelled world economic growth. Moore's law describes not just an anecdotal manufacturing phenomenon but a driving force of technological and social change, productivity, and economic growth.

A parallel implication of Moore's law is rapid obsolescence. As technologies continue to rapidly improve, the advances are often significant enough to render predecessor technologies obsolete.

In March 2001, American author, computer scientist, inventor, and futurist Raymond "Ray" Kurzweil proposed "The Law of Accelerating Returns," in which he wrote, "An analysis of the history of technology shows that technological change is exponential, contrary to the common-sense 'intuitive linear' view. So we won't experience one hundred years of progress in the 21st century; it will be more like 20,000 years of progress [at today's rate]."

Kurzweil took a long-range view of human history. "The first technological steps—sharp edges, fire, the wheel—took tens of thousands of years. For people living in this era, there was little noticeable technological change in even a thousand years. By 1000 AD, progress was much faster and a paradigm shift required only a century or two. In the nineteenth century, we saw more technological change than in the nine centuries preceding it. Then in the first twenty years of the twentieth century, we saw more advancement than in all of the nineteenth century. Now, paradigm shifts occur in only a few years' time. The World Wide Web did not exist in anything like its present form just a few years ago; it didn't exist at all two decades ago."

The Effect on Misalignment

In the previous chapter we discussed misalignment and how it can be very costly.

The accelerating rate of change is important because it has the effect of *amplifying* misalignment and making it worse.

Think about a car on the highway. Traveling at thirty miles per hour, if the driver sees an obstruction a half-mile ahead—an obstruction is a type of misalignment between goal and reality—the driver has one minute to make a correction or stop the car.

At sixty miles per hour—a higher rate of change—the driver has thirty seconds to respond.

At ninety miles per hour, twenty seconds.

In a NASCAR race car traveling at 180 miles per hour, the driver would have just ten seconds to get out of danger.

In a jet aircraft traveling at 300 miles per hour, to avoid an obstruction a half-mile ahead the pilot needs to respond within six seconds.

We're not just talking about external threats like an obstruction in the road.

Imagine a baby strapped in a car seat. Suddenly the baby starts crying—really loud. Babies do this; it's a fact of life. The crying baby makes it impossible to drive the car. You need to quickly pull off the road and soothe the baby (that is, correct the misalignment between goal and reality!).

At thirty miles per hour, it might take you five seconds to safely stop your car.

At ninety miles per hour, it might take you fifteen seconds to safely stop your car. And you might be so distracted by the crying baby that you inadvertently zoom past your exit!

The faster you're going, the more quickly you need to respond to get back into alignment.

No matter what line of business—technology, consumer products, banking, pharmaceutical, entertainment—this new reality requires a fresh approach to not only developing a strategy but managing its execution. The strategy must be clear and based on real-world results and revenue goals. It needs to be in perfect alignment with itself and able to keep pace with the accelerating rate of change in the world. Organizations are subjected to enormous stresses—both internal and external—and fault lines are quickly revealed. To survive and thrive in today's economy, you need to be both organically whole and able to adapt to an increasing rate of change.

The Agile Approach

On that fateful April night, the *Titanic* was steaming through the night at a rate of about 21 knots, or 24 miles per hour. When the obstruction was spotted dead ahead, the ship could not respond quickly enough to avoid a collision. The misalignment between goal and reality became fatal.

If any single word could be used to describe the *Titanic*, it would *not* be "agile." The huge ship sailed straight ahead on its predetermined course, and when conditions changed, it couldn't recalibrate quickly enough. Its failure to complete its mission was a combination of human intransience and design shortcomings in the ship itself.

In business, the word "agile" has a specific connotation. The agile management approach is a direct descendant of a project management methodology that has its origins in the software industry. In fact, its introduction in the software industry is well documented and can be pinpointed to a particular time and place.

In February 2001, seventeen software developers met at the Snowbird, Utah, ski resort. Their intention was to discuss and analyze various project development methods. During the course of the meeting, they wrote the *Manifesto for Agile Software Development*. Some of the manifesto's authors went on to form the Agile Alliance, a nonprofit organization that promotes software development according to the manifesto's principles and values.

The Agile Manifesto reads, in its entirety, as follows:

> We are uncovering better ways of developing software by doing it and helping others do it. Through this work we have come to value:
> - Individuals and interactions over processes and tools.
> - Working software over comprehensive documentation.
> - Customer collaboration over contract negotiation.
> - Responding to change over following a plan.
>
> That is, while there is value in the items on the right, we value the items on the left more.

There you have it: a simple declaration of sixty-eight words that would impact not only the software industry but the broader world of business management. What managers in other industries soon realized was that these four elements, and the twelve principles that form their foundation, could be adapted for use in many areas of organizational management.

A key principle of agile methodology is the regular adaptation to changing circumstances. This does not mean that you throw away your business plan. Far from it! What it means is that your strategic plan, which may be intended to chart your course over the next year or five years, is not set in stone over the entrance to your building. It is not adopted with great fanfare only to be shoved into a dusty filing cabinet until its "sell-by" date has expired.

Think of a project strategy as the course charted for a crossing of the Atlantic by a big luxury liner. Of course you need a plan; to leave port without a detailed plan would be foolhardy. But as you encounter wind and currents, you need to constantly recalibrate your course. And if you should encounter an iceberg, you may have to make a massive adjustment and even reconsider your goals. Anyone would agree that it would have been better for the *Titanic* to have arrived a few hours late in New York than to not arrive at all.

Like a ship navigating through waters full of icebergs, getting to your objective and safely delivering your passengers can't be accomplished by sailing in a straight line. You'll need to change course often, a task made more complicated by two additional risk factors: the icebergs are in motion, and what you see on the surface may be only a small portion of the massive bulk that lies under the surface. The threats facing you are both mobile and difficult to quantify.

As you progress on your voyage, your long-term objective may not change, but the path you take to get there will.

In business, close daily cooperation between business people and customers fosters a climate of agility, whereby the company is never caught off-guard by an unexpected external or internal change. Communication is often enhanced by a networked dashboard system that delivers a common inventory of timely information to every team member or stakeholder who needs it.

Agile product design methodology transformed the business of software development and implementation. To the design and delivery process it brought the idea of *functional iterations*. No longer does a software client expect a fully finished million-line piece of code to be delivered like a gift with a bow on top; nowadays, the process is iterative, with the customer involved in every iteration. The finished product is one whose components have been thoroughly pre-tested. It's durable and it conforms to the *current* requirements of the customer, which might have changed since the initial order was placed.

The agile approach brought tremendous benefits to software development, and the same methodology is gaining increasing acceptance in the wider arena of business management. CEOs and managers have discovered that the agile approach can transform an organization and bring measurable benefits. Here are just a few.

Improved Project Predictability

In business, surprises are never good. No one wants to go down the road of a project only to discover they're off course and need to double back. Avoidable mistakes that waste time and resources are often caused by outdated information. Agile project management incorporates practices and tools for improved predictability. Tracking individual project team speed allows management to predict timelines and budgets. Using the information from daily stand-up meetings and dashboard data allows the project team to predict performance for individual project segments.

Reduced Risk

Risk is something that you try to bend to your advantage. Nothing worthwhile comes without risk, but accepting unnecessary risk is both foolish and expensive. The agile approach mitigates risk by cutting down on the number of unknowns in any set of facts. In product development, when product iterations are short, market risk is reduced. Feedback from customers helps evolve the product and lowers risk of the product failing to match market expectations.

Agile techniques virtually eliminate the chance of total project failure by always having a working product, starting with the first iteration, so that no agile project fails completely. Constant internal feedback on projects through daily stand-up meetings and data provided by agile business software allows management to see and react to new conditions on a regular basis. The organization as a whole has greater flexibility for accommodating market changes.

Improved Ownership and Collaboration

Silos, turf wars, and ego-driven actions impede progress and stifle innovation. One of the essential characteristics of the agile method is the opening up of lines of communication both internally among individuals, teams, departments, and externally between company and customer. The management team, the customer, and the team members work closely together on a daily basis.

More Relevant Performance Indicators

The market moves fast, and no manager can afford to rely upon dated reports. The metrics that agile managers use to measure team performance, estimate time and cost, and make strategic decisions are more relevant and more accurate than metrics used on traditional projects. Agile management determines project budgets and timelines based on each team's actual performance and capabilities. Using real-time data, rather than reports generated at the end of the day or even weekly, allows an accurate assessment of an individual project team's knowledge and capabilities. Comparing the cost of future projects with the value of that future project helps management determine when to end a project and reassign resources to a new project.

Time management is critical. When you have to wait for a cumbersome report to be delivered to your desk, that's time wasted. When the R&D team has to wait for feedback from the customer, that's time wasted. The agile business environment, when supported by a digital dashboard system showing real-time key performance indicators, is finely tuned to respond quickly and decisively, and to ensure that every action moves the team one step closer to the goal line.

On the ill-fated *Titanic*, imagine what might have happened if during that long minute between the sighting of the iceberg and the impact, the person who had to make the instantaneous decision—in this case, First Officer Murdoch, who was on the bridge—had instantaneous data delivered to him regarding the effectiveness of his response. There's evidence to suggest that the response taken was not the best choice, but as the seconds ticked by, the first officer had no way of knowing this—the data slowly coming to him was inadequate.

Higher Team Morale and Productivity

The old-school method where management directives flow in a one-way stream from the C-suite to the front lines is rigid and self-defeating. Agile management promotes a free exchange of information and ideas in an environment of respect for both managers and employees. Being part of a self-managing team encourages people to be innovative and creative, and they expect to be acknowledged for their expertise.

The agile approach removes obstacles, and working cross-functionally allows team members to learn new skills and to grow by teaching others. Agile is a lean approach with no irrelevant documentation, no useless daily meetings, and fewer paper artifacts. Face-to-face meetings are productive and may even take the form of "stand-ups," whereby the physical act of standing up for the duration of the meeting encourages brevity. Agile teams self-organize themselves so that information is timely communicated to all stakeholders.

Higher Customer Satisfaction

An important goal of every business is simple: to meet the expectations of the customers. Every methodology and strategy, regardless of the name attached to it, must help the organization achieve this goal. Agile companies satisfy customers by keeping customers involved and engaged throughout the project cycle, and by delivering products to market quicker and more often with every release. Agile companies can be more efficient and productive, making not only customers happier but also their investors.

Lean Management

The concept of agility is also related to the idea of lean operations. During the late 1980s, a research team headed by Jim Womack, PhD, at MIT's International Motor Vehicle Program coined the term "lean" to describe the manufacturing practices at Toyota. The characteristics of a lean organization and supply chain are described in *Lean Thinking* by Womack and Dan Jones, founders of the Lean Enterprise Institute and the Lean Enterprise Academy (UK), respectively. The book describes the thought process and the overarching key principles that must guide your actions when applying lean techniques and tools.

Being lean is defined as the art of minimizing the amount of unproductive work and of unproductive investment. This means that energy is not wasted on activities that do not add value, and what is done is leveraged for maximum effect. Lean thinking changes the focus of management from optimizing separate technologies, assets, and vertical departments to optimizing the flow of products and services through entire value streams that flow horizontally across technologies, assets, and departments to customers.

Eliminating waste not merely at isolated points but along entire value streams creates processes that require less human effort, less space, less capital, and less time to make products and services at lower cost and with fewer defects. Companies are better able to respond to changing customer desires with high variety, high quality, low cost, and with fast throughput times. Also, information management becomes much simpler and more accurate.

In today's rapidly changing business environment, the old method of plan, execute, get results, and evaluate is no longer acceptable. To get to your destination safely, you need to be willing to question every step of the process and then go back and revise your strategy, your plans, and even your expected results quickly and repeatedly. The icebergs are out there, and they're in motion; to dodge them takes agility, a lean methodology, and the willingness to uncover those aspects of your strategy that are out of alignment, and then get them realigned.

3. Getting into Alignment: The Five Steps

Every stage of an organization's activities—from identifying the need to be served to delivering the product or service and then distributing profits to investors—needs to be in perfect alignment with the desired results, and every alignment needs to be adjusted as conditions change. When the *Titanic* set sail on Thursday, April 11, 1912, the ship's owners had done an admirable job of putting the enterprise into perfect alignment for success. The ship was state-of-the-art, the crew experienced, the course well charted, and the return on investment projected to be healthy. The people involved were pros who had done this many times before. Every contingency was accounted for—or so they thought. The metrics were sound. All of the foreseeable risks—including hitting an iceberg, which was not unheard-of in the transatlantic trade— were deemed to be manageable.

Even the number of lifeboats was acceptable, and for a good reason. The lifeboats were never considered to be the sole means of transport for *all* the passengers and crew. In the busy highway of the North Atlantic, if the ship were to become disabled, the lifeboats were designed to ferry passengers to a waiting rescue vessel. Indeed, if the *Californian* had responded to the *Titanic*'s distress call, this is exactly what would have happened: the ship's twenty lifeboats could have easily ferried all the passengers to the rescue vessel. Plus, the *Californian* could have dispatched its own lifeboats to assist in the ferrying operation.

The *Titanic* didn't sink because the company's strategy was flawed or poorly conceived. In actuality, it had been meticulously planned by experts, much like a transatlantic airline flight is today. When the ship sailed, the metrics were good. The ship sank—and the project was a disaster—because while changing external conditions warranted a rapid review and realignment, the people involved blithely stuck to the plan.

A rigid, inflexible plan is as bad as no plan at all.

At the end of the day, it all comes down to *people*. The people who make up an organization can either embrace agility and transparency or cling to their comfortable ways, fearing change.

So how does an organization get teams aligned on reality and make people feel comfortable sharing their frank but constructive opinions on the alignment to strategic execution?

As in any process of education, *understanding* how a process can work is the first step toward building confidence.

The Input and the Output

Imagine a deep pond. Extending across the pond is a series of stepping-stones. In order to get from one side of the pond to the other, you need to walk across the stepping-stones. The stepping-stones need to be in perfect alignment; otherwise, you won't be able to cross the pond. While you're walking across the pond—in either direction—if you miss one stepping-stone, you're going to fall in the water. To make the journey requires agility, alertness, and a focus on getting to your goal.

The place where you begin is your strategy, created by all the inputs that matter.

Your destination, across the pond, is the desired result, or the output.

In between are the stepping-stones. In order to guide and support you, they must be perfectly spaced and in alignment.

As we saw in the case of the *Titanic*—and with General Motors and countless other examples—while *planning* the placement of your stepping-stones is important, a willingness to *move them* as conditions change is equally important. If there's one thing you can rely on, it's that conditions will change. The water's current will shift your stepping-stones, they may sink in the mud, or a competitor may even steal one. You may need bigger stepping-stones to carry more weight as your business expands. Your destination may change too, which will require realigning the entire set of stepping-stones.

None of this happens by itself. There is no fairy godmother who will wave her magic wand to fix your stepping-stones. If a stone needs to be moved, you and your people need to do it. No one else can.

To help you visualize the journey from strategy to results, I have framed a go-to-market (GTM) model that illustrates the five primary stepping-stones that form your path:

1. Strategy
2. Plans
3. Activity
4. Funnel
5. Results

Within and between these five big stepping-stones will be lots of smaller steps, but these are the primary ones.

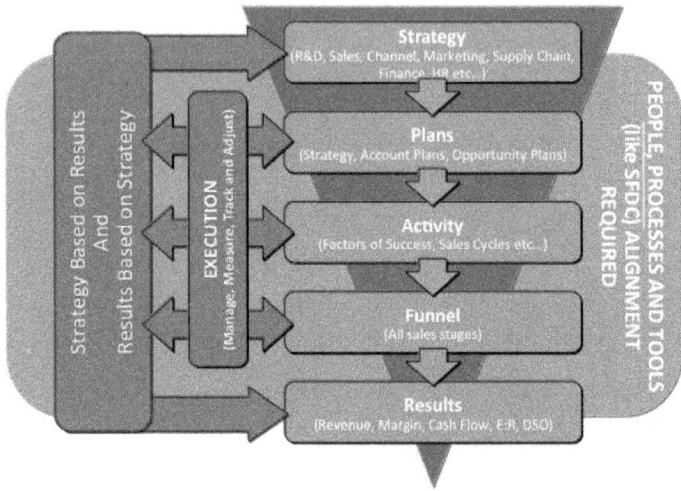

First, the stepping-stones look like a conventional ladder or waterfall. Strategy leads to plans, which lead to activity, which lead to a funnel, and then to results. This is an acknowledgment of the reality of the temporal framework in which we humans conduct our activities. We first strategize, then plan, then execute. This is the way it's been done for thousands of years, and we're not going to change that.

As I said earlier, getting into alignment is only the first step. It's an important step, but it's only the first one.

The key to agile management is the fact that the two ends of the ladder are connected.

Strategy leads to results.

Results lead to strategy.

When you first create a strategy, you do so with the goal or results in mind. You set a goal, such as, "We want to be number one in the US cell phone market within five years." Then you develop your strategy to accomplish this goal. You design your product and see how it performs in tests. You manufacture your product and sell it at an appropriate margin.

But as you work through the process, you're always checking to make sure that the path you've chosen:

1) Will get you to your destination, and2) The destination that you have chosen is still the one you want.

Question number two is not trivial. As conditions change, you may discover that the results you're striving for are no longer the ones you want and that you have to rethink your mission.

The case of Blockbuster Video shows how the game itself can change, and unless you're willing to rethink your goals, you might be out of business.

Blockbuster Video: Getting Out of Alignment

As proof of the adage "be careful what you wish for," in a world where the rate of change is accelerating, Blockbuster rose and fell with remarkable speed. At its peak in 2004, Blockbuster ruled the movie rental business with over nine thousand stores and sixty thousand employees worldwide. By 2010—only six years later—the company had filed for bankruptcy. Its upstart competitor Netflix quickly became the number one provider of movies to consumers.

Blockbuster started out with a fresh and brilliant idea. Founded by David Cook in 1985, the mission of the business was to take advantage of emerging DVD technology to serve customers who wanted to watch feature films at home. Cook realized that while consumers wanted to watch movies at home, they didn't necessarily want to *buy* the DVD of the movie; they were happy to rent it at a fraction of the cost. Blockbuster was like a lending library: it allowed consumers to rent videos of feature films, watch them at home, and then return the video to the store.

At the time, the idea was revolutionary. For the first time since the invention of network television in the 1950s, consumers were freed of the chains of network programmers. If you wanted to watch *Rocky Horror Picture Show* on a Tuesday afternoon, you could; all you had to do was rent the video from Blockbuster.

The initial success of Blockbuster was the perfect alignment of new technology, consumer demand, and scalability of the business. The company's strategy led directly to the desired results, and the results validated the strategy.

In 1987 the growing company was sold to Waste Management Inc. founder Wayne Huizenga for $18.5 million. In the same year, Blockbuster won a court case with Nintendo that paved the way for the rental of video games, opening up a huge new market for at-home gamers.

Under Huizenga's aggressive leadership, Blockbuster was soon opening a store every twenty-four hours as it sought to become the industry leader. The chain quickly grew to more than 2,800 stores.

In 1995, just ten years after the first Blockbuster opened its doors in Texas, Blockbuster Video was sold for $8.4 billion to Viacom Inc., the American mass media company.

Two years later came the event that has gone down in corporate history as a truly fateful moment. A customer named Reed Hastings was charged $40 for being late in returning the

DVD *Apollo 13*. Angry at what he considered to be unfair gouging, Hastings went on to create Netflix.

While it used exactly the same product as Blockbuster—the feature-film DVD—Netflix had a different strategy to deliver its product. It had no brick-and-mortar stores. Netflix had a website, which was launched on August 29, 1997, with only thirty employees. DVDs were available for rent through a traditional pay-per-rental model, and customers made their choices online. The DVDs were mailed to customers via the US Postal Service. Two years later Netflix introduced the monthly subscription concept and eventually solidified its business model of flat-fee unlimited rentals without due dates, late fees, shipping and handling fees, or per-title rental fees.

In the year 2000, in another moment that will go down in corporate history, the still-fledgling Netflix was offered to Blockbuster for $50 million. The company didn't see it as a good investment and declined the offer.

That same year, Blockbuster collected an astounding $800 million in late fees, making up 16 percent of its revenue for that year.

In 2002, Netflix went public. Two years later Blockbuster separated from Viacom and belatedly launched an online DVD subscription. Despite having nine thousand stores globally and being worth around $5 billion, the company was already hopelessly behind the new industry leader, Netflix. For the next two years Blockbuster flailed about, looking for a way forward. Several CEOs came and went, and the company made multiple changes in business strategy, which included abandoning the total access online service in favor of continuing the in-store, retail-orientated model. This decision ultimately left Blockbuster far behind its online rivals.

As Blockbuster, having rammed the iceberg, began to sink, Netflix stayed agile. In early 2007, Netflix began to move away from its original core business strategy of mailing DVDs and realigned itself by introducing video on demand via the Internet. As DVD sales fell, Netflix continued to grow on the Internet.

In 2010, Blockbuster filed for bankruptcy.

Today, the big question asked in every MBA classroom is, "Why didn't Blockbuster colonize the Internet the way it colonized suburbia?" Companies like Blockbuster had customer expertise, sophisticated inventory management, and strong brands. Why, like the *Titanic*, did it stubbornly hold its course?

The problem for Blockbuster was that it allowed its strategy to become fatally misaligned with what their customers wanted, and which they could get from Netflix. Blockbuster's huge investment, both psychologically and literally, in physical stores and physical DVDs made it slow to recognize the importance of the Internet. Blockbuster was late on everything—online rentals, streaming video, and Redbox-style kiosks. In the late 1990s—the heyday of the DVD era—customers had few alternatives and tolerated the chain's exorbitant late fees and absence of good advice about what to watch. Once Netflix emerged, suddenly customers enjoyed tremendous variety, were able to keep the DVD for a few extra days without draining their bank accounts, and got useful advice from the Netflix computer algorithms.

When the technology of Internet streaming became well established, the DVD—which had been revolutionary in 1985—quickly became obsolete. Netflix realigned itself, and as of October 2015, Netflix reported 69.17 million subscribers worldwide, including more than forty-three million in the United States. The rate of change was rapid indeed.

A significant reason why Blockbuster did not get itself into realignment was because of its company culture: Its leadership consisted of people who got rich when bricks-and-mortar stores were hugely profitable and who couldn't believe that those days were disappearing. The familiar sunk-cost myth made the situation worse: Once decision makers heavily commit to a project, they're likely to keep pouring *more* money into it, because of the investment already at stake. Rather than making a massive and painful realignment in the size and number of its stores, Blockbuster kept sailing full steam ahead toward the iceberg.

What happened to Blockbuster is a good example of *loss aversion*.

As first demonstrated by Amos Tversky and Daniel Kahneman in economics and decision theory, loss aversion refers to people's tendency to strongly prefer avoiding losses as opposed to acquiring gains. Since people prefer avoiding losses to making gains, this leads to risk aversion when people evaluate an outcome comprising similar gains and losses. The leaders at Blockbuster were averse to accepting unavoidable losses (getting rid of physical stores and the expenses associated with the decision) in exchange for gains from an alternative strategy.

A concept related to loss aversion is *status quo bias*. This is an emotional bias that takes the form of a preference for the current state of affairs. The current baseline (or status quo) is taken as a reference point, and any change from that baseline is perceived as a loss.

Status quo bias interacts with other nonrational cognitive processes such as loss aversion, existence bias, endowment effect, longevity, mere exposure, and regret avoidance. Experimental evidence for status quo bias is seen through behavior in regard to choices made by successful enterprises—whether Blockbuster Video or White Star Line—in which the status quo is preserved because of loss aversion.

Blockbuster also misjudged the character of its customers. In 1985, its pricing strategy was based on the belief that DVDs—then a new technology—were rare and valuable items. A customer was likely to steal the rented video or keep it around the house indefinitely, and therefore late fees had to be steep and swiftly enforced.

When Netflix started its DVD-by-mail idea, no doubt the people at Blockbuster thought the upstart company was crazy. You're going to *mail* someone a DVD and expect them to mail it back? But customers did mail the DVDs back, and the system worked.

Like the Titanic, Blockbuster began with a strategy that was in perfect alignment with its goals; but as conditions changed, the decision makers chose to avoid loss and stay on the predetermined course until the inevitable disaster occurred.

It is worth noting that Netflix's strategy adjusted from DVD to streaming, and they outpaced revenue declines from DVDs with the new paradigm of streaming. Not only were they more agile than Blockbuster, they applied agility to adjusting their target to continue to thrive.

4. Crafting the Strategy

When you talk about alignment, by definition you're talking about two or more elements in a set. You can't align one thing with itself; you need to align it with something else. Then you can align those two things with a third element, and so on.

If any one element in your aligned set gets out of whack, it can knock the others out of alignment too.

When you're starting out, you need to assemble all of the relevant pieces and get them into alignment. These pieces might include—but not be limited to—your goal, your financing, your human resources, your market, and your expected margin.

Broadly speaking, you now have a business strategy.

The word "strategy" derives from the Greek word "*stratēgos*," which derives from two words: "*stratos*" ("army") and "*ago*" ("leading"). A business strategy is a long-term leadership plan designed to achieve a particular goal or set of goals or objectives. It is a summary of how the company will achieve its goals, meet the expectations of its customers and investors, and sustain a competitive advantage in the marketplace.

Without a strategy, management has no roadmap to guide them.

Creating a business strategy is a core management function. How you define your business strategy will determine the direction of your business and what it will look like in the future. By defining your business strategy clearly, you can develop your business or growth plan to achieve your business and personal goals.

Once defined, your business strategy sets priorities for the company and management team, and helps you attract and retain the talented workers you need. Although each department in your company may focus on different priorities to accomplish specific tasks, these priorities need to be in perfect alignment with the overall strategic direction of the company.

Your business strategy should answer these questions:

- What's the company's mission?
- What's our core competency?
- What's our target market?
- Which products or services should we offer to fulfill our mission and make a profit?

As we saw with the example of the *Titanic*, your strategy must not be carved in stone. It must be subject to review and revision as conditions change. If you see an iceberg up ahead, you may have to alter your plans and change course. Will this affect your strategy and even your goals? You won't know unless you verify. If you have to increase your speed to make up for lost time, how will this affect your fuel costs? Will there be increased wear and tear on the engines? Will you have to pay the coal shovelers in the engine room overtime because they're shoveling more coal?

While it may seem expensive to adopt an agile posture and willingly change your execution and even your strategy as conditions change, sticking blindly to a preconceived set of plans can be even more costly. It can also be disastrous to change plans and implementation without reexamining your strategy and even your expected results.

Since a flexible business strategy is foundational, let's take a closer look at the components of a strategy: metrics, focus, differentiation, and execution.

Metrics

A business metric is a quantifiable measure that is used to track and assess the status of a specific business process. It's expressed as a number, a ratio, or a descriptive word and should also include time, like this:

- "Our goal is to get a 15% return on our investment."
- "We need to sell 60,000 widgets this quarter."
- "When a customer calls, a call center operator needs to pick up the call within eight seconds."
- "We want our new product to capture 20% of the Southeast Asian market within six months."
- "The average response on our customer service surveys should be 'highly satisfied' by the end of the year."

The word "metric" refers both to *the thing being measured, the resulting number*, and *time*. Therefore, while the things being measured—such as return on investment, or time required to respond to a customer inquiry—won't change over time, the results will change; and it is these results that you analyze and act upon.

Business metrics are employed to inform key audiences surrounding a business, such as investors, customers, employees, and executives. Some organizations provide business metrics in mission statements, which require buy-in from all levels of the company, while others incorporate them into their general workflows. While the primary goal of business metrics is to track movement, the overall point of employing them is to communicate a company's progression toward a set of defined short- and long-term objectives.

To be effective, business metrics need to be compared to established benchmarks or business objectives. This provides context for the values used in the metric and allows business users to better act on the information they are viewing. For instance, while $50 million in sales may be an impressive number for a small business, if you were Walmart, this number would have you wondering who forgot to add more zeros.

To be meaningful, an organization's strategy must be rooted in metrics that are tangible and predictable. Most leaders understand that. You cannot hit a target that does not exist or that is soft and left to the perception of the individual, the market, or the organization.

Metrics need to be developed carefully and reexamined often. This process requires the input of key stakeholders in the business as to which metrics are important to them. Every area of business has specific metrics that should be monitored: sales teams monitor new opportunities and leads, marketers track campaign and program statistics, and executives look at big-picture financial metrics.

Once adopted, the set of metrics should be retained over time to provide a comparison with past performance. For example, you won't know if your current margin is an improvement over last year's unless two things are true: you have last year's results, and the method used to determine the results this year was exactly the same as the method you used last year. (Some unscrupulous companies, in seeking to make their current numbers look better than they are, make changes in their accounting methods and bury the changes in the fine print at the end of the annual report. Doing this could be considered accounting fraud.)

Business metrics are different from key performance indicators (KPIs) in that metrics are used to quantify and track all areas of a business, whereas KPIs specifically target certain areas to gauge performance.

It is important to understand how metrics drive financial statements and the valuation of an organization. The accounting equation states that *assets equals liabilities plus retained earnings* and is represented as a balance sheet; the net effect of operations (*revenue minus expenses*) is the income statement; and the cash flow reports the flow of funds and the impact to the balance sheet and income statements. When targeting a metric it is important to understand how that metric will impact each of these statements. If you have a firm understanding of metrics, feel free to skip the next section.

Examples of Key Business Metrics

Here are just a few of the many metrics that are expressed either as numbers or as ratios.

Sales revenue is the income generated from all customer purchases minus the cost of returned or undeliverable items. It is the "top line" or "gross income" figure from which costs are subtracted to determine net income. Revenue can be calculated by multiplying the price at which goods or services are sold by the number of units or amount sold. Sales revenue must be in alignment with costs, and produces the gross margin (below).

Gross margin is calculated as a company's total sales revenue minus its cost of goods sold, divided by the total sales revenue, expressed as a percentage. The higher the percentage, the more the company retains on each dollar of sales to service its other costs and enjoy as profits. Retailers use margins because you can easily calculate profits from a sales total. If your margin is 20%, then 20% of your sales total is profit.

Tracking margins is important for growing companies, since increased volumes should improve efficiency, lower the cost per unit, and increase the margin.

The margin must be in alignment with the business model. For example, if your business is selling donuts, which require virtually no research & development costs, your margin should be much lower than a pharmaceutical company, which must carry higher margins to pay for the development of new drugs.

Overhead costs are fixed costs that are not dependent on the level of goods or services produced by the business. They include salaries, insurance, and rents being paid per month. Because overhead costs are not influenced by how much your business earns each month, you need to track them separately and diligently. Switching utility suppliers or moving to a location that is less expensive are ways to bring the fixed costs of running a business into alignment with revenues.

Variable costs are expenses that change in proportion to the activity of a business. Fixed costs and variable costs make up the two components of total cost. These include the "cost of goods sold" and other items that increase with each sale, such as the cost of raw materials, labor, shipping, and other expenses directly connected to producing and delivering your goods or services.

If your variable costs go up at the same rate as your sales, your business won't grow, even if revenue increases and the number of customers increases. The ratio of cost to revenue should improve as your volume grows. This is called scaling. A scalable business is one that can be expanded while the proportion of costs is lowered. Let's say you have an assembly line that can produce one thousand widgets per day. If you doubled your output to two thousand widgets per day while only increasing your costs by 50 percent, you've scaled up your business. But if your costs also doubled, you haven't scaled up your business; you've only made it bigger.

Cost of customer acquisition measures the total cost associated with acquiring a new customer, including all aspects of marketing and sales. Customer acquisition cost is calculated by dividing total acquisition expenses by total new customers over a given period.

Churn rate focuses on how many customers are lost in a given period and the cost to replace them. It's seen as a solid indicator of a rising cost of customer acquisition and a lowering in the customer's lifetime value to a company.

Customer loyalty and retention measures how long customers keep buying in a long-term, profitable relationship. A loyal customer will also act as an ambassador, spreading positive word of mouth. To improve service offerings and foster loyalty and retention among the customer base, companies gather feedback from customers via surveys, direct responses in store, or other types of analysis.

Inventory size is the business's assets that are ready to sell or will be ready to sell at any given time. Businesses must constantly keep track of inventory to account for how much product they have to sell, which represents their primary source of revenue. The amount of inventory must always be in alignment with how much it costs you to maintain that inventory and how much you expect to sell. For example, as gas prices soared in 2004, Detroit's automakers, faced with big inventories of unsold SUVs, ratcheted up discounts on their largest and least fuel-efficient models in hopes of moving out a glut of unsold pickups and sport-utility vehicles. Meanwhile, Toyota, which had kept its inventories and product mix more closely aligned to the anticipated rise in fuel prices, didn't have this problem.

Productivity ratios determine how productive a company's employees are. They are calculated by dividing a department's actual revenue by the number of employees, and then comparing that number to various industry statistics to gauge the effectiveness of staff. This metric can be applied to almost any aspect of the business. Measuring staff productivity is important; if you don't know how your staff is doing, then you can't truly know the inner workings of your own company.

An area of growing concern is the increasing misalignment of wages and productivity. The productivity of American workers continues to grow at a much faster rate than their compensation. From 2000 to 2014, American workers' total productivity increased 21.6 percent, while the median worker's compensation, including pay and benefits, rose just 1.8 percent. This divergence is a key contributor to the widening income gap that has put increasing political pressure on employers—and may create problems for companies that don't respond.

Profit & loss (P&L) is one of the three primary financial statements used to assess a company's performance and financial position (the two others are the balance sheet and the cash flow statement). The P&L statement summarizes the revenues and expenses generated by the company over the entire reporting period. It's also known as the income statement, statement of earnings, statement of operations, or statement of income.

The basic equation on which a P&L statement is based is *revenues minus expenses equals profit.*

Too often, metrics are overly complex or are not communicated in a way that everyone in the organization can grasp them. Even things as seemingly simple as "top line" and "margin" require a real exchange, allowing all in the organization to understand what they mean. Examples are often a good tool to crystallize these with the organization. You can use home finances as a means to demonstrate these targets. For example, "top line" is how much your family earns (before any withholdings). It's also known as sales (or whatever the term is for your organization).

It's important to recognize how certain metrics can exert pressure on individual and organizational performance. For example, a common method of executive compensation can create misalignment between executive decisions and the long-term health of an organization. Since the mid-1990s, the portion of executive pay that comes from stock options has steadily risen. At the time, academics, investors, and politicians, tired of seeing CEOs take home fat paychecks for poor performance, pushed to have stock options become a primary method of compensating executives. In theory, granting an executive the right to buy the company's stock tomorrow at today's price would pay off only if the company's stock increased in price. To advocates, options were the ideal solution that would align the interests of executives with those of shareholders. Boards granted bountiful options in part because, until recently, accounting rules meant companies didn't have to treat this form of compensation as an expense.

But the practice increased pressure on executives to make decisions that would drive up the stock price in the short term, and even created incentives to artificially inflate reported earnings in order to keep stock prices high and rising. Thus was created a misalignment between the desire to impress the market today and the necessity of making investments for the long term.

As long as we're talking about executives, it's important to add that too many executives inflate their egos by ensuring the jargon they use is not understood by colleagues and subordinates. Sounds silly, doesn't it? Think for a minute about some of the finance individuals you know. Their value is based on a superior understanding of how a company achieves and reports results. I cannot tell you how many conversations I have had with senior finance personnel in which they make a simple thing sound complex, and after an hour of "cross examination" you realize, with frustration, the simplicity of the conversation was masked by jargon and ego.

Here's an example from my personal experience. A friend of mine was once promoted to the position of senior vice president in charge of constructing leasing and finance options for institutions. At this new level on the executive ladder, she was concerned that she would not be able to comprehend the seemingly complex conversations to which she was being exposed. After about an hour of studying basic double entry accounting and the breaking down of the accounting equation and how everything flows into the balance sheet, income, and cash flow statements, my friend realized all of the jargon was tied to that core and was not insurmountable. In fact, she became so good at translating "complex finance speak" into plain English, she excelled at her job simply because many of her colleagues were unsure of what certain terms meant.

While business finance can be complex, the basics are often simple. Regrettably, in too many cases executives use "smoke and mirrors" to obfuscate a costly misalignment that has been allowed to grow out of greed, stubbornness, a belief that "this is always how we've done it," or a simple lack of understanding that the obfuscator doesn't want to admit.

Focus

The scope of what is offered by an organization needs to be clear and well defined. When setting strategy and developing plans, it's critical to define the core competencies of an organization. Be specific: What is the central set of competencies or solution(s) the organization will focus on? If you are in a large and/or diverse organization, I recommend sharing how each line of business works with the other (or does not). Getting this right is essential to success.

If a corporation is too rigid it will miss market transitions; if it's too loose, investment will be allocated with little or no return. If it's too broad, the equity may be spread too thin to reap the optimal return; too narrow and there will be excess that could have been allocated to other initiatives.

A now-classic example of a company losing focus is General Motors. Once the world's biggest automaker, through the last decades of the twentieth century the behemoth lost market focus across the dozens of different levels in the company that included the portfolio of divisions, brands within divisions, models within brands, the cosmetic and physical variations among models, market segments, dealers, and suppliers. A major problem with GM was a deeply embedded and long-held misconception about the real meaning of market focus and its critical connection to cash flow creation. For too long, GM's financial metrics focused on growing market share and revenue rather than on creating and sustaining positive net cash flow. The loss of market focus on the scale and scope of GM's led to huge cash losses and cascading effects that impacted all the other levels. The corporate, multilevel, cross-portfolio loss of market focus had a devastating effect on the capacity of GM to generate positive net cash flow. One example was GM's Saturn Division, a perennial cash flow loser that drained the company's assets and energy from 1985 until GM finally pulled the plug in 2009.

GM's legacy of annual cash losses even during high-growth boom years left it with little or no cash to deal with the downturn of 2008. The company ran out of cash, desperately sought government support, and eventually declared bankruptcy, from which it emerged—stronger and more focused—in 2010.

Unlike the *Titanic*, which failed to change course quickly enough and was fatally damaged, GM survived its impact with the iceberg. For example, in a rare instance of market prescience, in 2007 GM began developing the electric Chevy Volt, and its introduction in 2010 put GM in a leadership position for electric vehicles. The Volt won several industry awards, including the 2009 Green Car Vision Award, 2011 Green Car of the Year, 2011 North American Car of the Year, 2011 World Green Car, and 2012 European Car of the Year.

You're probably wondering if the Volt is a profitable product for GM or a loss leader. While R&D costs were significant, in early 2015 GM said the 2016 Volt 2.0 would indeed be profitable to sell, as the developers behind the car had found a way to subtract $10,000 in costs per vehicle. This would also make it easier to buy one, as the MSRP of the 2016 Chevrolet Volt was expected to drop significantly compared to the outgoing model.

As GM learned the hard way, and as we will see in future chapters, no target is stagnant, and all targets must be revisited as external forces or buying patterns demand. The focus and allocation of resources must be rooted in fact and data and devoid of emotion, politics, and ego. We will explore how facts can be made available, and how rooting decisions in those facts, and without emotion, politics, and ego, is often more an art than a science.

Differentiation

In nearly every market, consumers have no shortage of choices. No product or service remains unchallenged; as soon as a new and unique product is developed, competitors rush to introduce their own versions. In today's hypercompetitive business environment, you need to know what it is that your organization can do better than anyone. Is your organization an innovator, attracting "first adapters" who want to try something new? Are you a low-cost leader, catering to consumers who buy on the basis of cost? Are you offering a high degree of reliability, such as L.L. Bean, who will accept for return any item purchased from the store at any time?

Be honest, because masking this or stating it to be something other than it is can be a fatal error and result in a strategy based on flawed information.

Often this will translate into pricing and price elasticity calculations. Pricing is a core part of any strategy. Although not always as simple as cost plus a margin, many organizations revert back to this model in lieu of a better set of data.

In larger and/or diverse organizations, metrics, focus, and differentiation may vary by each line of business, group, or geography. It is important to outline how each of these components may vary from, or contribute to, the overall organization's strategy so all are clear how success is defined and how it is measured.

However, it is even worse when it is not rooted in an executable plan with clear dates, owners, and a process by which results can be monitored to confirm or adjust the execution plan or strategy itself.

Take, for example, the smartphone market. It's become huge and intensely competitive. As of this writing, the top ten global players are Samsung, Apple, Lenovo, Huawei, LG,

Xiaomi, ZTE, Coolpad/Yulong, TCL/Alcatel, and Vivo. If you were the CEO of a smartphone manufacturer, how would you differentiate your company? What unique value would you offer your customers?

You'd make this decision by understanding what customers want (even if they don't know it yet!) and what your competitors are offering. Every smartphone offers a blend of features; no smartphone can deliver all of them at one time. For example, you're not going to get a phone with the lowest cost combined with the most memory and best video capability. It just can't happen. If you offer the lowest cost, you must sacrifice some aspects of performance.

Some of the variables that enter into the buying decision include:

- **The wireless carrier.** The wireless service provider is one of the customer's most important decisions. No matter which device they buy, it's useless unless they have solid wireless coverage. Because each of the national carriers sells a wide variety of phones, choosing the service provider is the customer's first move.

- **The platform.** Right now, Google's Android and Apple's iOS are the two top smartphone platforms, both in US sales and in availability of third-party apps. Android sales have surpassed the iPhone, and Android's open-source nature makes it a tweaker's favorite. Meanwhile, Microsoft's Windows Phone has a solid, easy-to-use design and Microsoft's strong backing on the hardware side.

- **Apps.** For many people, apps are the primary reason they get a smartphone. Apple's App Store leads with more than a million apps, but Google Play is catching up quickly. Many independent app developers like the freedom offered by Google Play, but not all apps run on all Android phones.
- **Aesthetics.** Touch screens allow for slimmer devices, easy Internet browsing, smoother user interfaces, and a quality video-playback experience. On the other hand, while hardware QWERTY keyboards are easy to type on, they either add weight with their horizontal and vertical sliders, or they reduce screen size.
- **Cost.** Plenty of cell phones sold in the US are basic non-smart flip phones, including waterproof phones, texting phones, and ordinary voice phones. There are many reasons a customer would want a simpler, less expensive device. Unlike smartphones, feature phones don't need annoying software upgrades or to run thousands of additional apps. For voice quality, individual phones can vary in reception, transmission quality through the microphone, earpiece sound quality, and side-tone (the echo of your own voice that helps prevent you from shouting at the other person). Some phones have louder or clearer speakerphones than others.
- **Cameras and music players**. Many of today's top smartphones offer eight-megapixel (or greater) cameras, upgraded optics, and enhanced software for snapping and even editing surprisingly good

photos. For some customers, recording broadcast-quality video is important. Most of today's higher-end smartphones offer high-definition recording. Consumers buy products to fill a wide variety of needs. No product or service can fulfill every need. Therefore, to attempt to please everyone is a fool's errand. Make sure that the need you are serving is in alignment with the product you're offering, your sales message, and your cost basis. If your customers' needs change, you need to revisit your strategy and, if necessary, realign every functional area of your enterprise to meet those needs.

- **Incumbent Advantage.** As outlined earlier, loss aversion can be applied here too. Take Apple's music, apps, and the investment in time to understand the interface as an example. This creates a material hurdle for other players to motivate users to their offering.

5. Identifying the Gap

The enemy of perfect alignment is the "gap."

I'm not talking about the popular clothing store. I'm talking about misalignment that can be present in your go-to-market project or operation. A gap can be a slight sliver of a crack or it can be a yawning chasm that threatens to swallow everything you've worked for.

What you need to remember about gaps is that they do not heal themselves. Organizations are not like human bodies, which have the ability to repair themselves without you making a conscious effort. (At least when you're a little kid this worked well—it seems that as we get older, the miracle of self-healing takes a lot longer!) When gaps appear in an organization that is dynamic and striving for a goal, and which has lots of moving parts, they often don't get better by themselves. They fester and grow. To be corrected, they need to be identified, their danger assessed, and action taken.

Gaps can take many forms. Here are just a few big ones:

- In 1998, two companies that had vastly different corporate cultures—Chrysler and Daimler-Benz—tried to merge. The culture gap was never seriously addressed, and the merger ended in an expensive failure.
- At General Motors in 2005, engineers wanted to replace a defective car ignition switch at a cost of an additional 90 cents per unit. The finance people said

no, it would cost too much. The gap in priorities led to a huge recall of thirty million vehicles, 124 deaths, and billions in expenses for the company.

- In 1977, Kodak filed a patent for one of the first digital cameras. The technology used a magnetic cassette to store images. But Kodak was making so much money on film that it didn't introduce the digital system to the public. Even when it became clear the market was moving to digital, Kodak continued its focus on short-term profits with traditional film cameras. When Kodak finally got into the digital market, it was too late—the gap had grown into a chasm.

- In 1999, a Mars orbiter that had cost $125 million was lost in space. The reason? When building a critical component, the engineers at Lockheed Martin, the builders of the Mars Climate Orbiter, had used English measurements, while the NASA team had used metric ones. The misalignment prevented navigation information from transferring between the spacecraft team at Lockheed Martin in Denver and the flight team at NASA's Jet Propulsion Laboratory in Pasadena, California.

- In 2012, a disagreement between Apple and Google led Apple to yank Google Maps as the default mapping application on its iOS products and replace it with their own. Unfortunately, Apple's mapping system wasn't nearly as good as Google's. Locations were mislabeled, some streets weren't shown, and it occasionally provided wrong directions. The problems were eventually resolved, but it was an embarrassing blunder for a company known for never launching a product before it was perfect. The lesson to be learned? No matter how desperately you want a product to get to market, never release it until you've tested it and it meets every expectation.

In each of these cases, the gaps developed *over time*. They started out small and, because they weren't promptly identified and fixed, they got bigger. At Apple, the supersmart software engineers must have known their new mapping software wasn't ready to compete, and their top priority was probably product quality and performance, but the marketing guys had a different priority—their goal was to get rid of Google and make a quick substitution. That's two conflicting goals, and the gap was eliminated only after Apple suffered a painful blow to its prestige. As Jean-Louis Gasée wrote in *The Guardian*, "One is left to wonder how such a hot issue, Apple maps v Google maps, wasn't handled with more care—before the blowup. And why, with inevitable comparisons between an infant product and a mature, world-class one, the marketing message was so lackadaisically bombastic. And last, the CEO. Was trust in his team misplaced or abused? Were the kind of checks that make Apple's supply chain work so well also applied to the maps product, or was some ill side-effect of team spirit at play, preventing the much-needed bad news to reach the top?"

It's All About the Flow of Information

Once you've embraced the idea that gaps are bad and must be identified and corrected, the logical questions are, "Where do you start? What's critical to the process? What's the most important first step?"

The answer is that you first need accurate, reliable, and timely information.

Let's go back to the *Titanic*. It's true that the plan to cross the Atlantic was inflexible and its implementation was "by the book," right up until the last minute. It's true that the ship had design elements—the lifeboats, the structural steel, the propellers—that had not been perceived as *flaws* because no contingency was imagined that would expose their inherent weaknesses. In hindsight, you could try to make the case that the *Titanic* was a disaster waiting to happen, but in fact at that time there were a dozen similar luxury liners crisscrossing the Atlantic that never had an accident, much less sank to the bottom.

What we can say with absolute certainty is that if the *Titanic* had received critical information a few minutes earlier than she did—perhaps even a few *seconds* earlier—she could have easily steered clear of the deadly obstacle in her path. The immediate and primary cause of the tragedy was poor information. Every other factor was secondary.

Likewise, if the engineers at Lockheed and NASA had known that they were using different scales of measurement, they might not have lost a $125-million-dollar satellite.

If the people at Chrysler and Daimler had known of the huge cost of the culture gap between the two companies, they might never have attempted a merger.

If Kodak had realized that it was in the *image* business and not in the *film* business, it might have become a leader in digital photography.

Gaps can exist in every area of your business, and the first step toward erasing them is to have accurate information. Earlier in this book we talked about the accelerating rate of change. Nowhere is this more evident than in the area of the collection and processing of information, especially as it trickles up to the decision makers. In the old days—that is, the 1990s and before—information came to a decision maker in two ways:

1. Data

The first way consisted of data in the form of *numbers*. Sales numbers, costs, margins, defects, market share—all the metrics and key performance indicators. Generally, the data would be generated daily, weekly, or even quarterly. There were always time lags—gaps—between when a number was generated, when the leader saw it, when the leader took action, and when a result was seen.

If a new product was launched, leaders might not receive hard data on sales for days or weeks. Think back to the days of Christopher Columbus. He first set sail for the New World on August 3, 1492. His patrons—King Ferdinand and Queen Isabella of Spain—had to wait for *seven months*—until Columbus returned in March of 1493—to learn whether their investment had been a success.

2. Reports

The second way a leader got information was through *reports* from subordinates. The information could be oral or written, and could encompass any topic relating to the business. Reports were often delivered at the weekly staff meeting. It's a scene familiar to anyone in business—the CEO would sit at the head of the conference table and say, "Okay, now let's hear from marketing. How's the new product rollout going?" And then the marketing guy would give his report.

One problem with reports from subordinates is that if there was ever an unsatisfactory way to receive unfavorable news—which, after all, should be the most *valuable* kind of news—it's from people who want to impress the boss. No one who's ever been in business needs a lesson in the enthusiasm with which subordinates lie to their superiors.

Employees either omit the truth or offer a falsehood for a number of reasons—some innocuous and others more serious. They include:

Desire for personal gain. Employees use deception to discredit other employees and make themselves look better within an organization. They may exaggerate the amount of hours they work, provide overoptimistic forecasts of projects they know will do poorly, or blame outside vendors or partners for failures. In fact, in one meeting I recall a projection that would require each person in the US population to buy three of the product; it seems the compounding growth and the personal gain sought was not bound by the addressable market.

A belief the system is corrupt. To survive, some employees believe it's necessary to bend the truth. They think the culture is one of "the survival of the fittest," and you can't be an honest person and climb the corporate ladder.

Avoid responsibility for setbacks. For whatever reason, employees don't do what they're supposed to, so they cover up their lack of performance. This form of deception is prevalent in complex organizations where coworkers can easily deflect blame away from themselves without directly implicating another person. If a project fails, a person in R&D can vaguely blame "the people in accounting" without accusing an individual. I always guide teams that bad news early is good news!

Personality issues. Sadly, some people are poorly equipped to function well in a group. Some tell white lies to avoid looking bad or upsetting someone. The problem may not be consciously created; it can sometimes be characterized as a mismatch of communication styles. One employee may be all too willing to give her boss bad news, while another may think that he or she needs to solve the problem by themselves and not burden their superior.

Not all reporting problems are caused by employees. Especially in the old days, reporting took time, as we saw in the example of Christopher Columbus. Actually, in the whaling business during the nineteenth century, an incredibly long reporting time was routine. In 1851, the average length of a whaling voyage from New England was *forty-six months*. That meant if you were a ship owner, you'd invest in the voyage and send the ship off to distant lands—and pray that nearly *four years later* your investment would pay off with a full load of whale oil! Until then, you had only scraps of information and rumors from other returning ships to give you any clue as to how your project was faring. Today, even a stalwart "buy-and-hold" investor like Warren Buffett would blanch at such a time frame.

Some gaps in time are simply part of the system, and even

short gaps can be critical. On April 14, 1912, the wireless room of the *Titanic* had received several warnings about icebergs in the area. The last warning was received at 9:40 p.m. For reasons unknown, this warning was never delivered to the bridge. (It would have been carried by hand on a piece of paper.)

The first hard information about the iceberg was obtained by the lookouts at 11:40 p.m. For the next minute, a series of fatal gaps in time worked against the ship. The first gap in time—a few seconds—occurred when the lookouts rang the bridge on the telephone to report the iceberg. The second gap was when First Officer Murdoch delayed giving the order to change course—he wasn't sure that the ship was actually on a collision course. The third gap was the steam-powered mechanism that took up to thirty seconds to turn the rudder. The fourth gap was that the ship's massive engine had to be manually reversed in the engine room, costing more time. These gaps—which individually were of little consequence—added up to a fatally slow response.

Today, digital technology has changed the game for every business leader, from the owner of a fleet of ships to the guy who runs a small business out of his home office.

Business Dashboards

Gaps are dangerous and need to be closed. You can get back into alignment using three tools: speed, information, and the will to make change.

Business dashboards can provide the first two. The third— the willingness to change—is up to the "art"—you and your team.

Business dashboards take their name from automobile dashboards because their function is similar. Under the hood of a typical car, there are dozens of processors and sensors that generate digital data about the performance of the vehicle. The car's dashboard summarizes this data and presents it using visualizations so the driver can quickly get the information he or she needs to safely operate the vehicle.

The business dashboard does the same thing: it collects data from selected sources, gives it context, and displays it on a computer screen in a way that's easy to understand. They work by connecting application programming interfaces (APIs) with the business systems in use. Among others, these systems include accounting software, customer relationship management (CRM) systems, the company email system, website analytics program, sales reports, and more.

The executive dashboard pulls all this information into one place so the leader doesn't have to log into multiple systems. It can also manipulate this data so the information is in a more accessible format.

Putting data into context is extremely important.

In today's business environment, the tendency is toward more data; but data by itself is meaningless. Extracting real value from raw data is a key challenge facing any decision maker. Data needs to be transformed—by editing or interpreting—into actionable information. For example, knowing that sales were $1.5 million last quarter may not tell you much. But placing that data point into context makes it meaningful, such as: "Last quarter our sales were $1.5 million, which is 5 percent above the same quarter last year. The increase in sales came from our new marketing push to increase online sales."

That's information which is much more useful. A dashboard can display such information graphically—with a pie chart, for example—so that the decision maker can read it at a glance.

A well-designed dashboard is a critical information management tool. Dashboards simplify complex processes into manageable, digestible chunks of information so that leaders can focus on the day-to-day operations of the business.

Not all dashboards are the same. They can be broken down according to the type of information they provide, and can be said to be strategic, analytical, operational, or informational.

Strategic dashboards support managers at any level in an organization, and focus on high-level measures of performance and forecasts. With static snapshots of data (daily, weekly, monthly, and quarterly) that are not constantly changing from one moment to the next, they provide the long-range overview that decision makers need to monitor the health and opportunities of the business.

Analytical dashboards typically include more context, comparisons, and history, along with contextual performance evaluators. Analytical dashboards often support interactions with the data, such as drilling down into the underlying details. They may be more tightly focused in one operational area, such as finance or sales.

Monitoring dashboards often support monitoring of specific activities and events that are constantly changing and might require attention and response at a moment's notice. For example, a monitoring dashboard might be used by a facilities manager who needs to supervise the complex environmental systems in a large building.

An **informational dashboard** typically resembles a spreadsheet, with one or more column headers and one or more row headers, and displays measure values at the row-column intersections. Informational dashboards are also useful for stakeholders who may not be making decisions but who need to be fully informed about information sectors that are relevant to them.

As tools for interdepartmental activities, dashboards provide an objective view of current performance and can effectively serve as common ground for further dialogue. For instance, let's say that marketing and sales need alignment over the customer acquisition process. Dashboards can present metrics that are relevant to each team in a way that is mutually understandable.

In regard to the technology, the dashboard is certainly enhanced in accessibility (mobile) and usability (interfaces). However, it has become bigger than that. The dashboard can perform a wide variety of complex tasks. Here are the essential functions of an analytical dashboard:

1. Present Information

Data is the foundation of any dashboard, and the quality of the data is of critical importance. Bad data = useless dashboard = a poor basis for decisions. Since the days of Christopher Columbus, getting good, current data has been a challenge; in the digital era the task has been grounded in a complex process called extract transform load (ETL). The process has three stages and, while widely used, is not the way to run a railroad:

Extract data from multiple data sources. The proper extraction of data correctly sets the stage for the success of subsequent processes.

Extraction is often not a simple process. With multiple data sources, each separate data source may use a different data organization or format. Common data-source formats include relational databases, XML, and flat files, but they may also include nonrelational database structures such as information management system (IMS) or other data structures such as virtual storage access method (VSAM) or indexed sequential access method (ISAM), or even formats derived from outside sources by means such as screen scraping or web crawling.

An intrinsic part of the extraction involves data validation to confirm whether the data pulled from the sources has the correct or expected values in a given domain. If the data fails the validation rules it needs to be either rejected or transformed.

Transform the data for storing it in the proper format or structure for querying and analysis purposes. In the data transformation stage, a series of rules or functions is applied to the extracted data in order to prepare it for loading into the end target.

An important function of transformation is the cleaning of data, which aims to pass only usable data to the target. As we saw in the example of the Mars Climate Orbiter, among other things the process must ensure that the attributes of different sets of data are compatible—that is, you don't try to merge metric measurements with English measurements. If such a situation is encountered, the data must be made compatible. You never want apples and oranges—you want apples and apples. The process may therefore match and translate coded values, such as if one set of data is recorded in inches and another set is recorded in centimeters, the program will choose one and translate the other to match.

The process may select and match only certain columns to load. For example, if the source data spreadsheet for an ocean liner has four columns or attributes consisting of speed, distance, direction, and time, then the desired selection may take only speed and direction. The selection mechanism may also ignore all those records where there's no content, such as when the speed is zero, or null.

Sorting the data, ordering, joining data from multiple sources, aggregating, transposing or pivoting, splitting a column into multiple columns, disaggregating repeating columns, looking up and validating the relevant data from tables or referential files, and applying any form of data validation may all be a part of the transformation process.

Load it into the final target (database, report, or dashboard). The load phase loads the data into the end target—in this case, the dashboard. Depending on the requirements of the organization, some data warehouses may overwrite existing information with new information on a daily, weekly, or monthly basis. Older data may be incorporated into the current display (for example, a graphic showing the stock price of the company since its inception). Complex systems can maintain a history and audit trail of all changes to the data loaded in the data warehouse.

The dashboard can be directed to display only information relevant to the user. For example, a credit card company will share information on a customer among several departments, and each department will have that customer's information sorted in a different way. The accounting department might list customer Jones by a number, the membership department might list customer Jones by name, and the risk department might list customer Jones by his credit score. In the next chapter you we will explore how this is no longer an effective (results and cost) way to access and compile data, using a fly as an example.

2. Make Decisions

Atop the foundation of good and current data, there are often many decisions that can be made logically within set criteria or based on the impact of previous decisions in an iterative manner. There are business rules engines (BRE) and analytical solutions that can:

- Make decisions based on set criteria. For example, if demand falls 10 percent below current inventories, then stop manufacturing the product; or if above 10 percent, then increase production.
- Learn and make iterative decisions. The dashboard can have the ability to mimic logical thinking by making adjustments, monitoring results, and then in real time updating the business rules in an iterative way. For example, in an automated call center where a customer navigates a succession of menu choices before reaching a human operator, the system can monitor the interactive voice response (IVR) hold time and customer satisfaction vs. the cost of adding more human customer service reps. The system can balance these metrics and "learn" where the optimal

balance is based on business goals. For example, if customer satisfaction and cost reduction are optimally matched within certain parameters, then the system can find the target customer hold time that meets customer satisfaction goals while containing human payroll costs.

3. Communicate

This may seem like an obvious task that hardly needs mentioning, but how your dashboard communicates, and with whom or what it communicates, is becoming increasingly sophisticated.

The first way you'd assume your dashboard conveys information and decisions to you would be visually. You look at the screen and it gives you information. Very simple!

It may also communicate with sound, including artificial speech, like Siri and your turn-by-turn GPS genie do. Again, this is becoming familiar, even to folks who were born before we had personal computers.

6. Machine to Machine:
Gapless Communication

Do you know why it's so hard to swat a housefly?

Think about it. You see a fly on the table. Slowly raising your hand, you carefully creep closer . . . closer . . . closer. The fly sits there, seemingly oblivious. When you think you're as close as you can get, you slam the palm of your hand onto the tabletop.

Whack!

You raise your hand.

No fly.

He has blithely flown across the room.

How can a creature with a brain smaller than a grain of sand be so infernally quick?

It's because the compound eyes of the fly feed information directly to the muscles controlling the wings. The fly's response to take off is a *reflex*, not a conscious decision. It doesn't "think" about its choice to avoid the hand; it just *happens*.

Taken from nature, this is a primitive example of machine-to-machine communication (M2M). In the case of the housefly, the eye collects information and sends a signal to the wings, which become activated. There's no conscious operator in the loop. The goal of the housefly—to avoid being squashed—and its operational capabilities are in perfect alignment.

What's becoming increasingly widespread—and keeps futurists awake at night—is the rapid growth of M2M communications in every facet of human life. In an increasing number of industrial and even home applications, a computer is connected with a stand-alone device, and directs that device based on the information it has collected and the business rules that it's been programmed with. Except to provide oversight, the participation of the human operator is not necessary.

Some M2M applications are basic and familiar. For example, consider the humble thermostat on your wall. It contains a temperature sensor. When the sensor detects that the air temperature has fallen below a certain number, its preprogrammed business rules tell it to activate the furnace in your basement. The furnace starts, the air heats up, and when the air is warm enough, the thermostat tells the furnace to shut off. You, the human operator, are never involved. Unless you choose to intervene, you're out of the loop.

In this case there is no gap between the temperature falling below a preset level and the furnace turning on.

For a more sophisticated example, consider a driverless car. It's equipped with hundreds of sophisticated sensors that detect a wide range of variables, from the car's speed to the distance between the car and an obstruction. The data is fed in real time into a processor (or a group of processors), which, based on preprogrammed business rules, issues commands to guide the car. What are the business rules? There are thousands; a few might be:

"Between the car and the vehicle in front, maintain a distance of one car length per ten mph."

"At an intersection, the red octagonal sign indicates a full stop of two seconds."

"If an object approaches rapidly from the side, brake to avoid a collision."

Basically, they're all the same things you learned in Driver's Ed. In a driverless car, all that you, the "driver," need to do is occasionally look at the car's dashboard to ensure that all systems are functioning well. If they are, you can go back to reading your newspaper or texting your friends. Just like in the case of the thermostat, the goal is to reduce the gap between a change in the environment and the car's reaction to zero. Most accidents are caused by human error; computers are becoming powerful enough to gather enough information, process it, and issue a command more quickly than a human.

You can only imagine the fate of the *Titanic* if she had been equipped with simple M2M systems that could have detected the iceberg and instantly ordered evasive action.

What does M2M have to do with the world of business and commerce, and staying in alignment to maximize profits? To find the answer, let's investigate a ubiquitous, unglamorous industry that's worth billions of dollars—the vending machine industry.

How M2M Helps Vending Machine Operators Stay in Alignment

The ubiquitous vending machine is a familiar sight in offices, schools, and public places. You know the basic business model: a freestanding box, often refrigerated, is stocked with any one of many consumer items—soft drinks, cigarettes, food, candy, snacks. You put your money into the machine, push a button, and your selection drops down into an opening where you can retrieve it. It's a big business; according to IBISWorld, the US vending machine industry today is worth $8 billion and comprises roughly twenty-four thousand businesses employing sixty-five thousand workers.

The sector is intensely competitive. External pressures on margins include food price increases from manufacturers and wholesalers, and consumer habits pushing snack purchases away from vending machines toward lower-priced outlets such as supermarkets and coffee shops. Traditionally dominating vending machine sales, consumers' appetite for candy, snacks, and confections is declining. This segment, which represented 30.2% of industry revenue in 2015, also includes potato chips, cookies, crackers, nuts, and other snacks.

The vending machine business is like any other retail business in that the operator needs to keep his miniature store—his vending machine—stocked with just the right mix of product to sell. Stale products, unpopular products, or empty slots result in lost sales or unhappy customers. Therefore, keeping each machine properly stocked and operating is a key operational goal.

How does this work in real life? Up until the twenty-first century, it was a simple and straightforward procedure. The field representative responsible for the maintenance and restocking of the vending machines would drive his truck from location to location, machine to machine. He'd pull up at the site, go inside, unlock the machine, open it, and visually inspect the contents. He'd count the product inside and replenish the items that were low or sold out. He'd remove the coins from the lockbox before recording his actions on a paper form attached to a clipboard. Then he'd close the machine, get back in his truck, and drive to the next location.

There would be times when he'd open a machine to find that it required only a few items, making the visit hardly worth his time. There would be other times when he'd discover that several selections were sold out, and he had no idea of how long the slots had been vacant. How many sales had been lost? It was difficult to tell. The best he could do was to replenish the sold-out items. When he returned to the main office, he'd file his paper report. The inventory manager would copy the field rep's report into a ledger (or, later on, a computer spreadsheet), and over time, trends would be noted.

Such as: "During the last two quarters the vending machine at the high school hockey arena has shown an increase in sales of pretzels. This has been accompanied by a decrease in sales of packaged brownies. We recommend taking two slots from packaged brownies and assigning them to pretzels."

You can see how difficult it was to keep *consumer demand* in perfect alignment with *inventory*. It was pretty much a guessing game, resulting in persistent expenses, both in lost sales and the cost of the traveling field representative.

But what if you could equip each vending machine with sensors to detect inventory levels and other data, such as the time of day when sales were most frequent? And then you connected the vending machine to a central processor that could inform the manager of the status of every product in every vending machine, in real time?

Actually, if you were to use twentieth-century analog technology it wouldn't be such a difficult task except for one thing: most vending machines are not easily connected to a landline telephone. To transmit the data, you'd need a wireless method of communication.

Enter the Internet of Things and wireless technology.

The Internet of Things (IoT) is the network of physical objects ("things") that are embedded with electronics, software, sensors, and Internet network connectivity. In the IoT sense, "things" can refer to a wide variety of devices such as "smart" vending machines, self-driving vehicles with built-in sensors, heart monitoring implants, biochip transponders on farm animals, or field operation devices that assist firefighters in search and rescue operations. These devices collect useful data with the help of various existing technologies and then autonomously flow the data between other devices.

British entrepreneur Kevin Ashton first coined the term "Internet of Things" in 1999 while working at the Auto-ID Labs; he was referring to a global network of radio-frequency identification (RFID) connected objects.

In fact, the humble vending machine was at the center of the concept of IoT. As early as the 1980s, the idea of a network of smart devices was discussed. According to popular mythology, the first Internet-connected appliance was a modified Coke machine at Carnegie Mellon University. In 1982, thirsty computer students wanted to know the inventory level of their local Coke machine. They wired up the Coke machine with microswitches to report on levels in the racks in the machine. Thus connected, it was able to report its inventory and the temperature of newly loaded drinks.

The Internet of Things is growing. According to a 2011 Cisco white paper by Dave Evans, IoT is defined as having emerged at that point in time when more "things" were connected to the Internet than people. Evans estimated that IoT was "born" sometime between 2008 and 2009, when the number of devices connected to the Internet exceeded the world's population of 6.8 billion people. Experts estimate that by 2020 the IoT will consist of almost fifty billion objects vs. a world population of 7.6 billion people.

Typically, IoT offers advanced connectivity of devices, systems, and services that goes beyond machine-to-machine communications (M2M) and covers a variety of protocols, domains, and applications. The interconnection of these embedded devices (including smart objects) offers automation in many fields while also enabling advanced applications like a Smart Grid and expanding to areas such as smart cities.

Additional examples of sensing and actuating are reflected in applications that deal with heat, electricity, and energy management—such as in vending machines—as well as home security solutions. With IoT, the electrical devices installed in your house can function independently of your control.

Within the context of the IoT, machine-to-machine applications typically consist of a *device* (a meter or sensor) that captures an *event* (temperature, inventory level). Information is then *relayed* through a network (wireless, wired, or hybrid) to a software program that translates data into meaningful information. For example, a data point of "Rack #2 contains three cans of soda" may translate into the actionable information that the soda cans in rack #2 need to be restocked, because rack #2 has a capacity of twenty cans.

In the early days of M2M, such communication was originally accomplished by having a remote network of machines relay information back to a central hub for analysis, which would then be rerouted into a system like a personal computer.

However, modern M2M communication has decentralized the old hub-and-spoke connection and changed into a system of networks that transmits data to personal appliances. The expansion of global IP networks has lessened the amount of power and time necessary for information to be communicated between machines. These networks also allow an array of new business opportunities and connections between consumers and producers in terms of the products being sold.

A good example of the deployment of smart vending machines is provided by beverage giant Coca-Cola. Since 1929, Coca-Cola has used vending machines to deploy products to satisfy the immediate needs of consumers. Innovations have paralleled advancements in electromechanical technology, and are now incorporating networked digital capabilities that have opened new opportunities to turn the traditional "dumb, unconnected" device into a "smart, connected" device. While Coca-Cola vending machines are ubiquitous, they, and competitors' machines, are increasingly placed according to infrastructure requirements that enable the networked digital capabilities to function.

Coke has a business-to-business (B2B) segment called CokeSolutions that positions and deploys vending as a managed services opportunity. The business value that smart, connected vending machines can deliver is aligned with the growing number of smart devices that consumers use, such as their smartphones used as mobile wallets.

The Freestyle is a touch-screen soda vending machine that offers the consumer the choice of more than 125 different

Coca-Cola drink products and custom flavors, which are then individually blended and dispensed. To further close the gap between the personal taste of the customer and what the company can instantly deliver, an enhanced "Create Your Own Mix" feature on the Coca-Cola Freestyle app allows users to create a custom beverage flavor mix of their own and then connect their smartphones to dispensers at participating outlets and pour it on the spot.

A network ID for each machine is essential for network connectivity, giving each machine the ability to be identified in space (location) and time. With its smart machines, Coca-Cola has taken an aggressive infrastructure position, reportedly acquiring sixteen million unique network IDs to use with its Freestyle vending machines as they deploy. Just some of the intended capabilities of networked vending machines include machine stock levels that automatically trigger replenishment orders, real time test marketing, and delivering third-party value offers to mobile wallets. The machine uses RFID chips to detect its supplies and to radio resupplying needs to other units. The machines transmit supply and demand data to both Coca-Cola and the vending machine's owner, including brands sold, times of the day of sales, troubleshooting information, and service data.

An important development has been to synchronize the vending machine with the mobile wallet in the consumer's smartphone. Coke machines in Japan have had this capability since the early 2000s, built upon Sony's contactless transaction chip, FeliCa, which was the dominant contactless format in Japan for the first decade of the twenty-first century.

In the United States, the first significant deployment of contactless payment-enabled Coke vending machines was announced in 2006, based on MasterCard's PayPass technology. This first effort was focused on taking a contactless payment for a Coke product in the vending machine.

Coke is also experimenting with gamification to allow customers to bond more closely with hundreds of thousands of its vending machines. Another ongoing experiment is the "peak shift" energy conservation vending machine which, when more broadly applied in other countries, will have an impact on smart city initiatives.

What does the use of smart vending machines mean from the perspective of alignment? It means that many costly gaps can be closed. They include:

- Lowering the cost of unproductive visits by a field representative.
- Increasing the number of machines one person can service.
- Lowering the cost of lost revenues when a vending machine is sold out. (If restocked promptly, a smart vending machine should *never* be sold out.)
- Tracking sales in real time to maximize the return on investment (ROI) of each machine (which, after all, is a miniature freestanding retail store).
- Providing customers with exactly the flavors they want, and tracking flavor popularity.
- Market testing new flavors at low expense and with little risk to the brand.

For example, here's what *CokeSolutions.com* said about the value of the consumer data that can be collected by a smart vending machine: "Recent Coca-Cola data show that the highest percentage of beverage, meal, and snack sales— thirty-five percent—comes between 10 a.m. and 2 p.m. Using that data, a vendor or merchant could conceivably offer specialized deals at the lowest traffic time—2 a.m. to 6 a.m.—in an effort to boost sales then. The data also reveal the possibilities of bundling. If the average customer buys a sandwich and regular soft drink, there's nearly a sixty percent chance that he'll also buy chips. So why not incentivize the chip purchase, driving that percentage even higher?"

With a smart vending machine connected to a dashboard, a manager could try out a special price for chips, and then see—hour by hour and day by day—if the offer has increased his margins. He or she could quickly fine-tune the offer to hit the sweet spot of depth of discount, sales volume, and profit margin.

For any business, this level of interconnectivity helps focus the entire organization on where customers transact or will transact. It's a way to capture deltas between *expected* results of strategy and *actual* results, and how to develop plans and activities to close those gaps.

It all starts with sales, opportunities, and the activities that drive those opportunities. Combined with accuracy of being able to forecast, one could argue that forecast accuracy of less than 10 percent is a sign that strategy and execution are out of alignment and the folks developing strategy don't have the control and impact they may think they do. In other words, in the case of a smart vending machine, the vast amount of real-time data it produces, if properly processed and acted upon, should enable the operator to forecast the chosen key performance metrics to within 10 percent. If for some reason this isn't happening, then the chosen metrics aren't the right ones or the operator lacks either the knowledge or will to take the obvious and appropriate actions suggested by the information produced by the machine.

Every day—and sometimes every *minute*—a company must take an honest look at what is happening in their organization, both behaviors and the results these behaviors drive (top-line, product/service mix, margin, customer satisfaction, etc.). Having an honest baseline of what is happening, why it's happening, and the behaviors driving the results will help develop the three key aspects of your strategy: metrics, focus, and differentiation.

Business Relevance

Many technology and services organizations aspire to be "business relevant." Something that is business relevant is capable of making a difference in the decision-making process. Data needs to have predictive value about outcomes past, present, and future. Information needs to be available in a timely fashion before it loses its value in decision making, and have feedback value that provides information about earlier expectations.

Just as there is a difference between data and information, statistical significance is not exactly the same thing as business relevance.

Statistical significance means that the measured result 1) actually occurred and 2) is not a random result. For example, if a company spends $80 million on a television ad campaign, and the measured result of the ad campaign is statistically significant (for example, a proven increase in new sales), then the marketing director can be confident that the campaign had an effect in the marketplace.

However, statistical significance says nothing about the *value* of the effect. For that, we need to quantify the business relevance.

Business relevance means that the magnitude of the effect is large enough to be important to the business owner. For example, if the $80 million television campaign generated $250 million in new sales, then under ordinary circumstances the campaign would be considered to have had a relevant impact on the business. Alternatively, if the $80 million television campaign generated only $30 million in new sales, then most marketing teams would conclude that the campaign had little business relevance.

Assuming that business relevance means having value statements that are transacted on beyond the IT organization, if the activities driving transactions are occurring between that organization and the CIO or their team, then by definition they are not business relevant. If business relevance is the goal, then one would expect the activities to center around, or at least include, line of business teams outside of IT.

It is important to note a "line of business owner or lead" is one that directly impacts a P&L for a reported segment of the business or a separately tracked business unit. This can also be referred to as a "profit center." Bear in mind, just because it is not IT does not mean it is a line of business. In addition to IT Human Resources, finance and facility are examples of cost centers.

In order to be effective, any strategy must be rooted on what *is*, not what one *wants it to be*. For example, if the organization thinks they are selling to a particular market segment and the reality is they are not, then any strategy based on selling to that segment will be flawed out of the gate.

Generally, marketing miscalculations can be very costly. But there's one recent example with a happy ending, at least for the company—the National Football League. For decades, just about everyone associated with professional football assumed that the audience for football consisted primarily of men. Men played the game, men watched the game, and men bought team apparel, like team-branded shirts and hats. When the guys gathered 'round the TV set on Sunday afternoon to watch the game—while wearing their team paraphernalia— their wives and girlfriends would huddle in the kitchen, emerging only to deliver bottles of beer or fresh plates of nachos to their menfolk.

In the first decade of this century, marketers in the NFL started to notice that women enjoyed wearing their boyfriends' team clothing. They began to realize that while little of the NFL's apparel marketing was *targeted* to women (there were a few token items produced in pink, which was assumed to be girly), women were avid *consumers* of authentic, male-oriented NFL apparel. The only thing holding women back was the fact that items like shirts were cut to fit men's bodies; on women, the boxy shapes were unflattering.

The NFL realized that its marketing efforts for NFL apparel were not in alignment with reality, and that it was potentially leaving millions of dollars of revenues on the table. The league responded with a new marketing effort aimed squarely at women.

Here's what *The New York Times* reported on August 25, 2010:

> Ladies, if you have ever wanted to wear strappy stilettos with your favorite football jersey, you are in luck. This fall, the National Football League will begin an advertising campaign encouraging you to do just that. The campaign, called "NFL Women's Apparel, Fit For You," takes an approach to marketing clothing that is meant to be both fashionable and sporty. And while jerseys and T-shirts for women have been available on Web sites like nflshop.com and in catalogs, this is the first time the league has dedicated a campaign to apparel for women.
>
> If the terms "fashionable" and "football jersey" seem contradictory, that may be because of the way jerseys have been made. The league has carried women's attire for the last ten years, but followed the "shrink it and pink it" philosophy of taking a man's jersey and making it smaller and, well, pink . . .
>
> "When I look at what women are wearing now, they are trying to be fashionable and yet show they are fit," said Mark Waller, the chief

marketing officer for the NFL, adding that the campaign aims for women ages twenty to forty who are active, family-oriented, and casual or avid fans of football.

In the early part of this century, female interest in the NFL was growing rapidly. According to research by the Nielsen Company, in February 2010 an average of 41.9 million women eighteen and older watched the Super Bowl—the most on record, and more than watched the Academy Awards that same year. Additional research by the NFL and Nielsen revealed more than forty-five million women watched NFL games each weekend.

The NFL planned to spend $10 million on the initial campaign. By all accounts, the league's push to capture the female market for apparel has worked brilliantly. As Kristi Dosh wrote in *ESPNW* in September 2013, "The NFL has seen double-digit growth in women's apparel for four consecutive years and says it has also added 30 to 35 percent more items to meet the increasing demand. The number has been boosted by the support from women with familial ties to the league who have served as ambassadors for the league's line, and even created lines of their own. Suzanne Johnson, wife of New York Jets owner Woody Johnson, has been involved with the NFL's line since its inception and also showed support for a new NFL line from Junk Food Tees (created through a partnership involving Kristin Cavallari, wife of Bears quarterback Jay Cutler), which debuted at New York Fashion Week."

The NFL continues to refine its program. As Maura Brannigan wrote on *Fashionista.com* in July 2015, Rhiannon

Madden, the NFL's director of consumer products, said, "Each year we get a little smarter about it, a little more sophisticated about it. We look at what's happening in the marketplace, what's on-trend, what women are wearing on the street, and also what women are wearing in stadiums. We take cues from our fans, as well as what's happening in fashion."

Madden said that the NFL works with a number of different partners to develop the NFL's ever-growing female market. "We're really looking at the individual consumers, since we have such a massive female fan base. Forty-five percent of our fan base is female, so we can't speak to them all the same way." The selection of women's offerings has grown to include plus sizes, maternity, and leisure-minded workout gear.

As the NFL found out, it's not only necessary to tally up sales figures but to drill down to the consumer behavior that drives transactions. It's not just the "what" but the "how" and "why" that matter. By leveraging a tool like *Salesforce.com* (SFDC), leaders in any business can inspect not just the forecasted numbers but the activities and contacts that are driving them. A representative sample will indicate what is really happening. Leaders can also see where transactions may be happening as they intend; by simply searching titles of contacts in the systems, they can see where activities are "hot" around business leaders and therefore find example and success stories from where results are in alignment with the goal of the organization. They can then learn from these and have them as input to scale to a broader strategy that drives real behaviors, activities, and results. Gathering this data for a fact-based foundation to build from is essential.

Another way to search out the truth in this example may be to require teams to quantify the value of their solution to their business unit leads at their customers. What business unit metrics and strategies are impacted by the solutions they sell? If they are working with this audience, this should be an easy thing that theoretically should already have been done. If, after inspecting these, they are not complete or obviously aligned to the business unit priorities (for example, cutting IT spend is not a business-unit-relevant metric, whereas top line, ROE, ROI, EPS, etc. may be), then an exercise like this, in this situation, would not only help baseline with data that is happening today, but will also help the issue start teams' thinking to remedy it.

If indications are that they are not selling to the business leader, the organization has at least three paths to explore in order to adjust their strategic execution plans.

Three Typical Strategic Execution Plans

1. They may realize they have a strength selling to IT and adjust their strategy to capitalize on it.
2. They may realize there is a material gap and that they need to create a plan to move toward the stated strategy (resourcing, training, and offer management).
3. They may bifurcate and have teams who sell to IT and others who are hired and trained to sell to business unit leaders.

No matter what path is selected, it's paramount that it's based on *reality* and not what an organization *imagines*.

Equally if not more important is realizing this is neither a fixed effort nor one that is ever complete. Often organizations will stop here or a new leader will come in, and all the good work will be allowed to wither. No matter what strategic execution plans are developed, they *must* include a documented, forecasted prediction of results. For each part of the strategic execution plan, the hypothesis of *what* results will be realized and *when* is critical. A critical step worth reiterating—as it is rarely done in practice—is documenting the hypotheses, having clear and unambiguous forecasted results, and setting up checkpoints to review.

Stakeholders need to understand that a well-thought-out but "failed" hypothesis is as valuable as a "successful" one. The heart of successful strategic execution is looking at how strategy has truly impacted results so that quick action can be taken based on fact, not opinion. This is how failure followed by adjustment leads to success.

Simple Case Study

Here's a simple case study.

You can pick any of the three strategic execution plans shown above. For this example, let's work with #3: "They may bifurcate and have teams who sell to IT and others who are hired and trained to sell to business unit leaders."

The strategic plans may be as follows:

Task	Expected Results	Timeline	Owner
BU Track			
1 – Recruit, hire, and train teams to call on Business Unit leaders	10 individuals calling on BU leaders	6 months	Ima Trainer
2 – Create offers that align to this audience	Three offers that are researched to offer real and clear competitive advantage—aligned to key metric for BU audience	3 months	Jim Offer
3 – Teams call on BU leaders – Average sales cycle to date is 3 months Average deal size is $1M Average margin is 55%	10 booked deals sold to/through BU leaders Average sales cycle is 2 months Average deal size is $1.5M Average margin is 60%	12 months	Isa Hunter
IT Track			
1 – Train and create collateral specifically focused to help teams sell to this audience	All IT sales teams passing an exam that demonstrates they understand this audience and the value driver they may see in the company's offerings	6 months	Ima Trainer
2 – Create offers that align to this audience	Three offers that are researched to offer real and clear competitive advantage—aligned to key metrics for IT audience	3 months	Jim Offer
3 – Teams call on BU leaders – Average sales cycle to date is 3 months Average deal size is $1M Average margin is 55%	10 booked deals sold to/through BU leaders Average sales cycle is 2 months Average deal size is $1.5M Average margin is 60%	12 months	Isa Farmer

Another common example is pricing. Many organizations aspire to be the innovative leader and charge accordingly. Assuming this means their pricing, relative to competitive alternatives, can command and transact at higher rates if the activities driving results are around negotiation and ultimately result in significant discounts that in effect are *lower* than competitive alternatives, then by definition they are selling a low-cost solution.

J. Crew's Discount Dilemma

Everyone knows that the retail clothing sector is a cutthroat jungle that will devour all but the most nimble players. Correct margins and pricing are especially critical, because consumers have vast choices and can often postpone purchases until the price drops.

In June 2014, *Edited.com* blogger Katie Smith offered an analysis of the continuing problems at J. Crew, the venerable clothing retailer based in New York City. She wrote that in Q1 2014, the retailer had posted net losses of $30.1 million and a drop in comparable store sales of 2 percent. Company management attributed thinning margins to decreased store traffic and increased promotional activity,

Smith posed the question, "Was the initial price positioning wrong, or was the product at fault?"

One culprit may have been the high frequency of J. Crew's sales promotions, which taught consumers to wait and buy when pricey items were marked down.

Smith reported that at J. Crew, women's apparel had a discount rate of 52.5%, whilst menswear was at 43.3%

and kids a healthier 36.9%. The current US average was 43.9%, pointing to womenswear as a potential problem area for J. Crew. In contrast, Macy's rate of discounting was at 49.3%, Ann Taylor at 40.5%, and Nordstrom at 25.3%. Price slashes at J. Crew were broad as well as deep, with 10.9% of womenswear discounted by 40% or more.

The *spread* of pricing is also important—you need to offer something at every price point within your core market. At J. Crew, the categories where pricing was not evenly spread were dresses and outerwear, which were both underrepresented at the $200–250 mark.

Plotting the number of products discounted each month, across a year, suggested to Smith that J. Crew had created problems for themselves by discounting early in the fall 2013 season, with the highest number of discounts in the year being during September and October.

J. Crew regularly and aggressively marketed its discounts through its email newsletters. Smith found that in December 2012, twenty of that month's twenty-seven email newsletters promoted sales or discounting events. In December 2013, nineteen of twenty-six newsletters promoted a discount. In March 2013, sixteen of twenty-eight email newsletters promoted discounting. A year later, in March 2014, thirteen of twenty-nine email newsletters promoted discounting.

Which products you promote to consumers also matters. While J. Crew attempted a fifty-fifty split between full-price stock and sales promotions in their email communications, it appeared that they focused on the *wrong* full-priced stock. Looking at the full-priced items that sold fastest for J. Crew in early 2014, Smith saw a good mix of upscale garments.

However, these items were not well featured in the full-priced email newsletters, where simpler sports-themed items got precedence. J. Crew's upscale design-led pieces needed higher precedence, as they were J. Crew's point of difference in a market already crowded with affordable sweaters and jeans.

Smith concluded that the breadth of J. Crew's assortment was simply too great. J. Crew had overreached in attempting to appeal to too many. There were huge gaps between their core basic staples, their design-led seasonal offerings, and their J. Crew Collection range.

The cost of these gaps was a breakdown in consumer understanding of what the brand was and where its products sat. With the discount promotions coming in a steady stream, consumers were trained to associate the brand with good quality items that you could buy on sale if you waited.

The year 2014 ended on a dismal note for J. Crew. As *Fortune* magazine reported, "Most worrisome for J. Crew in 2014 was that its performance got progressively worse over the course of the year, culminating in a sales decline of three percent during the key holiday quarter. The biggest culprit? Dull women's fashions that the company had to clear out at bargain basement prices. By the holiday quarter, J. Crew's gross margin rate had fallen to 34.5%, not that far above that of a discount retailer like Target and certainly far from what a specialty store like J. Crew can command."

"Needless to say," CEO Mickey Drexler said on an investor conference call, "it's been a tough year for us and the numbers speak to that. The [retail] world was hugely promotional, giving goods away." Looking ahead, Drexler admitted that the company could ill afford another year with a net loss of

$657.8 million (on revenue of $2.3 billion) caused by massive discounting of fashions customers didn't want.

The company's troubles didn't go away. A year later—in June 2015—*The New York Times* reported, "The bigger challenge afoot is that while J. Crew in recent years moved up in pricing, the rest of the world shifted down. The rise of fast-fashion chains like H&M and Zara has improved the quality of low-priced goods, making J. Crew's more expensive clothes less appealing." Analysts said J. Crew's costly line was chasing away customers who frequented high-end department stores. Problematically, the strongest growth in the industry had been in the lower end. Discount clothing stores like T.J. Maxx and Marshall's were thriving. Where was J. Crew in the mix? It looked like a store with its base prices too high . . . and discounts that were too steep and too frequent. Consumers were trained *by the store itself* to wait until an item went on sale to buy.

Assuming it got its product mix in order, J. Crew may have been better off by maintaining realistic prices, offering fewer deep discounts, and selling discounted overstocked merchandise late in the season at clearly marked outlet stores.

7. Foundation #1: Technology

We've covered a lot of territory in this book, and while there will always be more case studies to examine and insights to discover, now is the time to circle around and zero in on the three foundations of Getting Stragile. We'll see how they're fused together to form an approach that, when applied consistently, will eliminate gaps between your strategy and your objective, leading to boosting the one metric that is the most important: your bottom line.

The Explosion of Business Data

From data comes information. The process of leveraging information and becoming stragile begins with access to vast amounts of data. Like never before in history, this has been made possible by advances in technology.

In 2013, Philip Evans, a senior partner and managing director at the Boston Consulting Group and the co-author of *Blown to Bits,* which is about how the information economy is bringing the trade-off between "richness and reach" to the forefront of business, gave a TED talk entitled "How Data Will Transform Business." He explained that since the 1970s, business strategy has been dominated by two major theories: Bruce Henderson's idea of increasing returns to scale and experience, and Michael Porter's value chain. As we enter the age of digital information, Philip Evans argued that a new force will rule business strategy in the future: the massive amount of data shared by competing groups.

The key is not just the amount of data that's growing, but the fact that an ever-increasing amount of digital data has an IP address. This means that it lives not in an analog book or even a digital CD, but on a server or personal computer. Data that has an IP address can be linked to any other data that has an IP address. This means that it's becoming increasingly possible to quickly *locate* and *extract* vast amounts of knowledge in order to see patterns and trends. If we run the numbers forward into the future, we see a steady multiplication in the stock of information that is connected via their IP addresses. Mathematically, if the number of connections we can make is proportional to the number of pairs of data points, then a hundredfold multiplication in the quantity of data is a *tenthousandfold* multiplication in the number of patterns we can see in that data.

Evans provided an example: In the year 2000 the first human genome, that of James Watson, was mapped as the culmination of the Human Genome Project. It took about $200 million and about ten years of work to map the three billion pairs of nucleotide bases.

Since then, the costs of mapping the human genome have dramatically declined. This phenomenon reflects Moore's law, which we discussed in chapter 2, describing a long-term trend in the computer hardware industry that produces a doubling of compute power every two years.

In fact, as of this writing, anyone can get a simplified "snapshot" version of their genome for less than one hundred dollars. Of the human genome's three billion base pairs, only several million are likely to differ from person to person.

Thanks to the genomic maps that the Human Genome Project made possible, by tracking which variants of those bases a person has, companies can sequence portions of these selected genomes for a relatively low cost.

For under one hundred dollars, companies such as 23andMe will provide you with certain key genetic information, such as your ancestry, without sequencing your entire genome.

In the days when mapping a genome cost millions, or even tens of thousands, it was basically a research enterprise. Scientists would gather some representative people, and they would see patterns, and they would try and make generalizations about human nature and disease from the abstract patterns they found from these particular selected individuals. But when the genome can be mapped, we open the door to genomic data being combined with other collections of data: clinical data, data about drug interactions, and ambient data that devices like our phone and medical sensors will increasingly be collecting. Think what can happen when we collect all of that data and put it together to find patterns we couldn't see before. Evans suggested that this could drive a revolution in medicine.

The Machine Intelligence Research Institute

When you combine big data with advances in computing power, what results is machine artificial intelligence (AI), a powerful tool that can close gaps between knowledge and action that have traditionally been unassailable. This power needs to be handled very carefully. Like Dr. Dave Bowman, the astronaut on his way to the planet Jupiter in the film *2001: A Space Odyssey*, will our trip become hijacked by our trusted computer, the HAL 3000, or will we remain in control of this monster we've created?

Many groups are trying to ensure we don't end up like Bowman, who, after a life-and-death struggle with HAL, had no choice but to unplug the machine. Based in Berkeley, California, the Machine Intelligence Research Institute (MIRI) is a research nonprofit studying the mathematical underpinnings of intelligent behavior. The organization's mission is to "develop formal tools for the clean design and analysis of general-purpose AI systems, with the intent of making such systems safer and more reliable when they are developed."

Researchers largely agree that in this century AI is likely to begin outperforming humans on most cognitive tasks. Given how disruptive domain-general AI could be, the group seeks to predict and shape this technology's societal impact. MIRI has made some predictions about the way forward:

- As perception, inference, and planning algorithms improve, AI systems will be trusted with increasingly complex and long-term decision making. Small errors will then have larger consequences. (In other words, even trivial gaps between strategy, methods, and expected goals could quickly grow into yawning and dangerous chasms.)
- Realistic goals and environments for general reasoning systems will be too complex for programmers to directly specify. AI systems will instead need to inductively learn correct goals and environmental models. (This speaks to the importance of agility, and

that the gaps will be so subtle and complex that the machine itself will be better equipped to detect and correct them.)

- Systems that end up with poor models of their environment can do significant harm. However, poor models limit how well a planning system can control its environment, which limits the expected harm. (Reality-based planning is essential. As they say in the computer business, garbage in, garbage out.)

- There are fewer obvious constraints on the harm a system with poorly specified goals might do. In particular, an autonomous system that learns about human goals but is not correctly designed to align its own goals to its best model of human goals, could cause catastrophic harm in the absence of adequate checks. (That is, if HAL doesn't understand the goals of his human designers and becomes confused, he may try to sabotage the mission to Jupiter.)

- AI systems' goals or world-models may be brittle, exhibiting exceptionally good behavior until some seemingly irrelevant environmental variable changes. This is again a larger concern for incorrect goals than for incorrect belief and inference, because incorrect goals don't limit the capability of an otherwise high-intelligence system. (Again, with HAL as the example, the computer functioned well enough until it was presented with an unforeseen challenge. In the movie, there were two backup HALs at the space headquarters on Earth, which performed normally.)

Stuart Russell, a MIRI research advisor and co-author of the leading textbook on artificial intelligence, argued in "The Long-Term Future of Artificial Intelligence" that we should integrate questions of robustness and safety into mainstream capabilities research:

"Our goal as a field is to make better decision-making systems. And that is the problem. [...If] you're going to build a superintelligent machine, you have to give it something that you want it to do. The danger is that you give it something that isn't actually what you really want—because you're not very good at expressing what you really want, or even knowing what you really want—until it's too late and you see that you don't like it."

IBM and Watson

No discussion of AI would be complete without talking about the real-life counterpart to the HAL 3000 in *2001: A Space Odyssey*. Developed by IBM, Watson is a question-answering computer system capable of answering questions posed in natural language. The computer system was specifically developed to answer questions on the quiz show *Jeopardy*. In 2011, Watson competed on *Jeopardy* against former winners Brad Rutter and Ken Jennings. Watson received the first-place prize of one million dollars.

(Incidentally, in wry swipe at Big Blue, the producers of *2001: A Space Odyssey* took the letters "IBM" and shifted them down one space to come up with the name "HAL." It's supposed to be an acronym for Heuristically programmed ALgorithmic computer.)

According to IBM, Watson can process 500 gigabytes—the equivalent of a million books—per second.

Let's put Watson into perspective.

In a 2015 interview for *Fortune* magazine, IBM Chairman and CEO Ginni Rometty said that we are entering a new technological era that marries digital business with digital intelligence. IBM calls it "cognitive business."

"Digital is the wires, but digital intelligence, or artificial intelligence as some people call it, is about much more than that," Rometty told *Fortune* editor-in-chief Alan Murray at the Most Powerful Women Summit in Washington, DC. "This next decade is about how you combine those and become a cognitive business. It's the dawn of a new era."

She told *Fortune* that there's a vast amount of information in the world, from the Internet to your computer hard drive, but nearly 80 percent of that information has been invisible to systems and computers—until now. IBM's Watson is symbolic of this era and is able to demonstrate the power of digital intelligence. Systems can now understand, reason, and learn.

There's still a long way to go before digital intelligence becomes the standard, but Rometty recommended five areas where a business can benefit now if it starts building a cognitive business:

1. Drive deeper engagement: Help clients behind the scene for better customer experience.
2. Scale expertise: Employee training is expensive, and this could be scaled more effectively.
3. Put learning in every product: Build products that adapt to each consumer's needs.

4. Improve operations: Streamline your supply chain to help margins.
5. Transform how you do discovery: From pharmaceuticals to financial industries, research will be the foundation of many segments in the future.

"Instead of being disrupted, be the disrupter. I do it inside my own business," said Rometty. "You will be the disrupter if you choose to do it."

IBM calls data "the new natural resource." We produce over twenty-five quintillion bytes of data every day, but 80 percent of it is unstructured. Watson applies its cognitive technologies to help change how we approach and understand this emerging wealth of unstructured information. It can ingest this unstructured data and not only understand it, but also reason about it, combine it with structured data, and learn from it. With every industry facing an explosion of data, cognitive solutions will change many aspects of how people learn and live, transact and relate, compete and win.

As a case study, IBM offers Comdata, a company in Brentwood, Tennessee, that provides innovative electronic payment solutions across industries, helping companies to manage spending and streamline operations. Comdata pioneered electronic payments for the trucking industry, providing comprehensive controls and data for managing fuel and other fleet expenses.

In a scenario reminiscent of the challenges faced by people who must travel to service vending machines, Comdata gives fleet operators tools to analyze their fuel expenses and highlight opportunities to cut costs. The company knew that the best way of promoting efficient spending would be to put real-time decision support information directly into the hands of drivers. The aim was to create a next-generation application that would combine fleet telematics and GPS information with Comdata's rich repository of data on fuel merchants, complete with real-time prices, twenty-four hours a day.

The cloud-based solution allowed truck drivers to decide where to stop for the best-value fuel, based on their current position, route, and timetable. The prices shown were personalized to each driver, automatically including discounts negotiated by their company, as well as personal preferences. Tom Pierce, Comdata's vice president fleet IT, said, "We can lead drivers to the location where their company will get the best price. IBM's Cloudant product has an impressive built-in capability to analyze routes and location geometry, and the inclusion of the fourth dimension—time—means that the app will not direct drivers to fuel stops that will be closed by the time they reach them."

8. Foundation #2: Science

The first step to becoming stragile is having the necessary tools needed to get the job done.

The second step is knowing how to use these tools effectively. This is the science of getting stragile.

It all begins with *data* (the raw numbers) that needs to be transformed into *information* (data that has context and meaning). Timely and accessible information is critical to identifying gaps and closing them. "You can't manage what you don't measure" is a venerable management adage that's even more relevant in today's competitive and fast-paced business environment. You can't manage for improvement unless you know what's hitting its goal and what's falling short. Without measuring something, you don't know if it's coming up short and if a better alternative exists.

Know What to Measure

Given the necessity of measuring performance areas, the logical first question is, "What should be measured?" It's not a trivial point. No one wants to waste time and resources measuring things that don't matter. You need to measure those activities or results that are important to successfully achieving your organization's goals. These are your key performance indicators (KPIs) that help your organization define and measure progress toward its goals.

Depending on the organization, key performance indicators will differ. A KPI for a software development company might be the number of defects in a million lines of code. A fulfillment department may have as one of its KPIs the percentage of customer orders shipped within twenty-four hours. A marketing business may have as one of its KPIs the percentage of its customers that are converted from sales leads.

What you measure depends on what the key drivers are for your business. To ensure its success, what does your business have to do absolutely correctly? For a cable television business—let's call it ABC Cable—key performance indicators for the marketing department might include the absolute number of households in a given community that are subscribers, the percentage of market share in a community, the total value of all subscriber contracts, and the value of the average contract.

Too much data can be overwhelming. If you attempt to measure too many indicators, there is a danger that you'll spend time focusing on areas that are not important to the success of your business. A flood of data will overwhelm actionable information.

It can be helpful to look at the available metrics as being like dozens of levers on a machine. Find the direct relationships that you can control with one lever, and then frame your hypotheses for what happens when it's pulled and see if it moves the machine. Needless to say, if you pull on a lever and it doesn't have any effect, then it's a pointless lever—or metric. Get rid of it or consign it to the bottom of a report.

When developing your key performance indicators, understanding your business model is important. You need to ask what products or services you sell, who buys them, why they buy them, and how you make a profit on the transactions. Generally, the two most important aspects of your business model are:

1. *Why* do people buy from you? What drives sales?
2. How do you make a profit from the transactions?

The first point—why people buy from you—is deceptively important because it cuts to the very reason that you're in business. For example, in the case of the cable TV provider the answer to the question: "Why do people buy from you?" is that people want news and entertainment delivered to their homes. This leads to the next question: "Yes, but why do they buy from ABC Cable and not XYZ Cable?" The answer is the company's unique selling proposition; in choosing a cable provider customers want reliability, choice of content, and low price. It's up to ABC Cable to accurately identify the correct mix and deliver it.

Point number two focuses on the ultimate reality of business: you must make a profit. Cash flow is important for all businesses. For example, measuring the average number of days you take to pay your accounts payable, the number of days to collect accounts receivable, and the number of times your inventory turns in a year can all help you determine your cash flow management.

Many companies track a slew of metrics. The issue is whether they are tracking the metrics that will identify how they are meeting the strategic needs of the company and if these metrics can reveal any gaps between strategy and outcome. If a metric cannot highlight a gap between strategy and outcome, you probably don't need it.

Know How to Measure

How you measure is as important as *what* you measure. For example, at ABC Cable, in the old days each outbound salesperson would manually tally their own calls and report the total to their manager at the end of their shift. This method is hopelessly inadequate because it's slow and prone to inaccuracy or even misrepresentation. The stragile choice is to use the appropriate software to track each outgoing call, measure how long it took the prospect to answer each call, record who answered the call, and measure how long the call took to complete.

Collecting the measurements in this way enables the manager to calculate the percentage of customer calls that are answered and converted to sales. It also provides additional measurements that help him or her manage toward improving the percentage of calls that reach qualified prospects. Knowing the call durations lets the manager calculate if some salespeople are chatting with prospects rather than being focused on selling.

These automatic measurements can be complete, accurate, current, and unbiased. The information can be made available to managers and team members in real time so that gaps between strategy and goals can be quickly identified.

If you're like most companies and have a small number of key performance indicators, you'll quickly realize that without some level of automation and a system to capture the data in real time, it will require significant manual effort to get the data that supports the compilation of these metrics.

How to Use Measurements

To paraphrase W. Edwards Deming: If you don't know how to use the measurements to improve your process, the calculations have been a waste of time.

Establishing key performance indicators is critical for driving continuous improvement in your organization. Every employee should be aware of how the company is performing against these key indicators, and be rewarded for their contribution in meeting or exceeding these goals.

The data should be available on a networked dashboard and presented in such a way that is easy to understand, is timely, and illustrates the overall trend of the company. Finally, these results should be used by key managers to drive decision making and improvements from the front line to the boardroom.

Measurements are often used as part of a continuous improvement plan, a concept that has been given a variety of names, including plan–do–study–act (PDSA), the Shewhart Cycle, the Deming Circle/Cycle/Wheel, and control circle/cycle. Regardless of the name, the goal is the same—to measure the key factors and improve them.

It's important that you communicate your metrics to all levels of the organization. The CEO wants to know what's going on, but the front line employees need to know also. They won't be motivated to improve unless they know how they're doing. In addition, many of the best suggestions on how to improve will come from front line staff who interact with customers.

Team and individual results can be disseminated using pie charts, line charts, key driver charts, and other graphs on the networked dashboard.

Review your metrics and use them to guide your decisions. With your metrics in place, you can tell which strategies are working and which aren't. If you make a change, you use the metrics to tell you whether the change has improved results. A decision maker must both understand the origins of the data and how it was manipulated. Each method of calculation has implications and limits, as do the sources of the data. To be relevant, the measures have to be understood by those using them. There are no magic formulas that guarantee success; only good management improves the odds against failure.

A Data-Driven Strategy

Having acquired an understanding of the difference between data and information, let's circle back to the data—the raw material from which actionable information is derived. Without robust data, you cannot hope to identify and correct damaging gaps.

A 2013 article by McKinsey & Company entitled "Three Keys to Building a Data-driven Strategy" hit the nail on the head. Authors Dominic Barton and David Court revealed that as data-driven strategies take hold, they will become an increasingly important point of competitive differentiation.

They proposed that to fully exploit data and analytics, three mutually supportive capabilities are required.

1. Companies must be able to identify, combine, and manage multiple sources of data.
2. They need the capability to build advanced-analytics models for predicting and optimizing outcomes.
3. Management must possess the willpower and authority to transform the organization so that the data and models yield better decisions.

These capabilities rest upon a foundation of two elements: the deployment of the right technology architecture and capabilities, and a clear strategy for how to use data and analytics to compete.

A clear vision of the desired business impact must shape the integrated approach to data sourcing, model building, and organizational transformation. Instead of asking what the data can do for you, determine what you want to do and then leverage the appropriate data to help you get there. Your goal should always be front and center, and your goal should always reflect the reality of your situation.

For example, the goal of the *Titanic* was to reach New York at precisely at dawn on Wednesday, April 17. Yet there were icebergs in its path. If slowing down or changing course to avoid the icebergs would have resulted in the ship arriving late to New York, then the solution would have been to increase the ship's speed to make up for lost time. If the ship were already steaming at top speed, then the ship's managers should have been willing to make the tough call: "We're going to be late docking in New York." Then, on subsequent crossings, the schedule would need to be "padded" sufficiently to allow for such delays. This could be done by either increasing the possible top speed of the ship or slightly reducing its normal cruising speed and adding a few hours onto the sailing schedule.

Regardless of the decisions made, the point is that the data is always the *servant* of the goal.

The Three Steps

Here are the recommended steps to ensure that data is aligned with the goal.

1. Choose the Appropriate Data

As we saw in the previous chapter, the universe of data is growing exponentially, while opportunities to deepen insights by combining data are accelerating. Bigger and better data give companies a view of their business environment that is both more granular and panoramic. The ability to see what was previously hidden improves operations, customer experiences, and strategy.

Companies may already have the data they need to tackle business problems, but managers don't know how they can use it to make key decisions. Companies can develop a more robust use of data by being specific about the business problems and opportunities they need to address.

One way to prompt effective thinking about potential data is to ask, "What decisions could we make if we had all the information we need?" External and new sources of data need to be carefully exploited. Social media generates huge amounts of unstructured data in the form of images, conversations, and video. Add to that the streams of data flowing in from sensors, monitored processes, and external sources.

Getting the necessary IT support is key. Managing unstructured data often remains beyond traditional IT capabilities. Legacy IT structures may not be capable of handling new types of data sourcing, storage, and analysis, and may prevent the integration of siloed information. While fully resolving these issues may take years, business leaders can address short-term big-data needs by working with CIOs to quickly identify and connect the most important data for use in analytics before launching a transforming operation to synchronize and clean up overlapping data, and identify gaps.

2. Build Models That Predict and Optimize Business Outcomes

Data is essential, but performance improvements and competitive advantage arise from analytics models that allow managers to predict and optimize outcomes.

Big banks know all about this. Ever since the Great Recession, the US Federal Reserve has compelled the nation's biggest banks to undergo annual stress testing. In these exercises, banks are required to model a variety of scenarios of future stress. For instance, one stress scenario might be "Ten percent of the mortgages held by the bank go into default." The requisite data is loaded into the computer and the results are revealed. If the result is that the bank is undercapitalized as a result of the scenario, the Fed can order it to increase its capital reserves.

The most effective approach to building a model usually starts not with the data but with identifying a business opportunity and determining how the model can improve performance. Companies should repeatedly ask, "What's the least complex model that would improve our performance?"

3. Strengthen the Company's Capabilities

A mismatch between an organization's existing capabilities and the emerging tactics needed to successfully exploit analytics can throw any modeling effort into disarray. Using big data effectively may require substantial organizational change, and three areas of action can help achieve this.

- Develop business-relevant analytics that can be put to use. Big data and analytics need to be in sync with a company's day-to-day processes and decision-making norms. Model designers need to understand the types of business judgments that managers make to align their actions with broader company goals. Open exchanges with frontline managers will ensure that analytics and tools complement existing decision processes.
- Embed analytics in simple tools for the front lines. Managers need transparent methods for using the new models and algorithms. While terabytes of data and sophisticated modeling are required to sharpen marketing, risk management, and operations, the manager needs a simple interface. Statistics experts and software developers may understand complex solutions, but frontline managers need intuitive tools and interfaces that help them with their jobs.
- Develop capabilities to exploit big data. Adapting and simplifying is a two-way street. Most organizations will need to upgrade the analytical skills and literacy of their managers who aren't software developers. To make analytics a part of daily operations, managers must understand that it's critical to identify

opportunities and solve problems. Adjusting individual mind-sets and organizational cultures may require a multifaceted approach that includes training, role modeling by leaders, and incentives and metrics to reinforce behavior.

Executives should act decisively to implement big data and analytics. Change should come through carefully targeted efforts to source data, build models, and transform the organizational culture. Flexibility is essential, since the information itself—along with the technology for managing and analyzing it—will continue to grow and change, yielding new opportunities. As more companies learn the core skills of using big data, building superior capabilities will become a decisive competitive asset.

9. Foundation #3: Art

Having acquired the technology and mastered the science of getting stragile, the third key is the art, which is about leadership, a deep knowledge of your business, and aligning and inspiring your people.

The art comes from you and your people. It's knowing how to leverage technology and science to their best advantage. It's about making 2+2=5.

A stragile business is a lot like a professional football team's offensive squad. The goal of the offensive team is to put the ball across the goal line. Pretty simple, right? The challenge is that the market—namely, the opposing defensive squad—is always changing and is ready to pounce on your slightest miscalculation. Because of the constant changes, your strategy for moving the ball downfield must be continually adjusted. It cannot remain static.

In this book we've been talking about gaps between strategy and goals, and nowhere else is this more starkly shown than on the football field. A gap of a split second can mean the difference between a winning touchdown pass and a wasted play. You've seen those spectacular eighty-yard touchdown runs? The chances are good that at the beginning of the run a defender missed a tackle by mere inches—and the gap between victory and defeat only grew wider as the unchallenged ball carrier sprinted downfield.

When to Call an "Audible"

Nowhere is the analogy between the business team and the football team more vivid than during the few brief seconds between the huddle—where the offensive play is called by the quarterback or the coach on the sidelines—and the snap of the ball that puts the play into action.

A lot can happen during those few seconds.

Here's a typical scenario. Every offensive squad has a set of plays that it can run. A team's playbook is a dense and intricate set of rules that every member of the offensive squad needs to have memorized. From the playbook, either the coach or the quarterback selects the next play to be run. Then the team goes to the line of scrimmage and sets up to run the chosen play.

Or not. Sometimes the chosen play isn't the one the team runs. When the ball is snapped, the offensive squad may execute a completely different play. On the sidelines, even the team's coach may be surprised.

After all that careful planning, why not stick with the preplanned strategy?

The change is made because the defense is flexible. The eleven defensive players on the field can set themselves up in a nearly infinite number of positions and combinations. Their defensive posture will change from play to play as they try to "read" the offense. This is the "market" in which the offensive team and the quarterback must succeed: ever-changing, aggressive, and always threatening. The slightest gap in execution by the offense will give the defense the opening they need to stop the play or even sack the quarterback.

Sometimes the defense—which is trying to guess what play their opponents will run—will set themselves up in a manner that effectively counteracts the chosen play. Sometimes they will set themselves up in a manner that exposes an unexpected weakness.

A good quarterback is able to "read" the defense—to look at a specific defensive alignment and instantly know if the chosen play will or won't succeed against it.

He does this by quickly scanning the key defenders and where they are on the field relative to the line of scrimmage. Their positions will tell him—among other things—if the defense is playing a *zone* defense or *man-to-man*. In a zone defense, a defender is responsible for a defined area of turf around him—his zone. If a ball carrier enters his zone, the defender is responsible for tackling him. If he's playing man-to-man, the defender has been assigned one opposing player to cover. No matter where that opponent goes on the field, it's the defender's job to stick with him and prevent him from receiving a pass from the quarterback.

Between the time the huddle breaks and the offensive line sets up for the play, the quarterback must read the defense. A typical defense consists of four positions: the big linemen, who are on the line of scrimmage and who generally don't change their positions; the linebackers, who set up just behind the linemen and who are called the "secondary"; the safeties, who are deeper downfield, behind the linebackers; and the cornerbacks, who patrol the edges of the field on the left and right.

A quarterback will typically look for the free safety, or the defender positioned deepest in the secondary, the part of the field behind the linebackers that the safeties and cornerbacks are responsible for. If the free safety positions himself considerably deeper downfield than the other defensive backs, he's probably playing a zone defense.

As he approaches the line of scrimmage, the quarterback also looks at the cornerbacks—the defenders who are positioned to the left and right of the defensive linemen. If the cornerbacks are positioned ten or more yards beyond the line of scrimmage, the quarterback will conclude that the defense is playing zone. If the cornerbacks are at the line of scrimmage, eyeball-to-eyeball with the offensive receivers, they're most likely playing man-to-man.

Knowing whether the defense is playing zone or man-to-man is important to the quarterback because he wants to know whether his potential pass receivers will be running through zones or chased by individual opponents.

If he discovers that the defense has guessed correctly and is properly aligned to stop the offensive play, the quarterback needs to call an "audible": that is, he can call out a different play. Since he's not in a huddle, he has to yell out the new play to his teammates, in full view of the opposing team and sixty thousand fans and millions of television viewers. Everyone will hear him.

Is this madness? Not if he yells out the play in code. (This brings us to the subject of corporate security and the protection of trade secrets . . . but that's another book!) Some components of the codes are ubiquitous and everyone recognizes them, while others are proprietary to the team. To make it even more difficult for the defenders, the quarterback may also yell out words or phrases that are deliberately meaningless.

For example, the quarterback may yell out, "756 Pump F-Stop on three." Here's how that translates into English:

756: The team has three receivers who are eligible to catch passes. These three numbers are the passing routes that the receivers should take. Every team numbers its pass routes and patterns, giving receivers clear instructions as to what routes to run. For example, route number 7 may be: "Run straight down the field and then make a 90-degree turn toward the middle of the field." On this play, the first receiver runs a 7 route, the second receiver a 5 route, and the third receiver a 6 route.

"Pump": This refers to the basic play and how the offense should line up on the field.

"F-Stop": In this particular play, the fullback can also receive passes. "F-Stop" is the code for the fullback's pass route.

"Three": Refers to the count on which the quarterback wants the ball snapped to him. In other words, the center will snap the ball on the third "hut."

After the quarterback reaches the line of scrimmage and puts his hands under the center, he yells, "Set," (at which point the linemen drop into their stances) and then something like, "Red seven, gold top, hut-hut-hut." The center snaps the ball on the third "hut."

In this case, "Red seven, gold top" means absolutely nothing. The quarterback says these words to distract the defense. But this is not always the case. Sometimes the quarterback's utterances at the line of scrimmage prior to the snap count inform his offensive teammates of how the play will be changed. The offensive linemen also know that the play is a pass because of the numbering system mentioned at the beginning of the called play.

Teams give their plays all sorts of easy-to-remember monikers such as Zoom, Buzz, Red Hot, Quick Ace. These names refer to specific actions within the play and are meant for the ears of the running backs and receivers. Each name (and every team has its own terms) means something, depending on the play that's called.

All of this happens in the space of a few short seconds. The ball is snapped and the play is run. With a little luck, the defense will miss something and the quarterback will find the gap and exploit it.

You may be wondering . . . What does all of this have to do with your business?

Plenty. On the football field and in business, success depends upon:

1. The ability of the individual team members to understand and retain large amounts of information (the plays and their corresponding codes) that relate to their positions. This goes directly to employee training. Your employees need to be well informed, capable, and empowered.
2. The ability of the coaching staff to analyze opponent behavior and use the information that is relevant. This goes to collecting data and transforming it into actionable information.
3. The ability of the quarterback or business manager to read the defense before every play.
4. The judgment of the quarterback or business manager in choosing an alternative strategy to close the gap between strategy and goal.

5. The ability *and willingness* of the team to listen to
    the quarterback, filter out the extraneous sounds
    (especially the nonsense words yelled by the
    quarterback to confuse the defense), and instantly act
    upon the new strategy without hesitating because of
    a personal attachment to the old strategy. This last
    point is of the utmost importance. Both on a football
    team and in a stragile organization, there's no place
    for ego. Imagine this scenario: You're a wide receiver.
    Your team is poised for the game-winning touchdown.
    In the huddle, the quarterback has called a play that
    means you'll be the primary target for his game-
    winning pass. In the eyes of the fans, you'll be the
    hero of the game. The huddle breaks and you go to
    the line of scrimmage. Suddenly the quarterback calls
    an audible. In the new play, you know you're just a
    decoy. You will not be passed the ball. You will not
    score the touchdown. Your teammate will be passed
    the ball and he'll score.

If you're a pro, none of this will make the slightest
difference to you. You'll execute the play exactly as you're
supposed to. When your teammates congratulate the other guy
for scoring the touchdown, you'll congratulate him too. All
that will matter is getting ready for the next kickoff and the
next series of plays.

Think about your own company. How often do egos
obstruct progress? Too often. Wouldn't it be amazing if
everyone were egoless and all that mattered was the success of
the organization? It would be the end of siloes, of withholding

bad news, of backstabbing, of petty rivalries, of jockeying for favor with the boss.

On a football team, the organization's attitude starts at the top, with the owners, then the coaches, and then the quarterback. It's the same with any organization. The company culture is set by those who control the levers of power. They must understand and embrace the art of stragile management. They must set the example for others to follow. They can have all the technology and science in the world, but without an understanding of the art, it will all be for naught.

Stragile Business Management

In football, stragile management is about market (defense) penetration, scoring more goals, and winning more games. In business, it's about establishing a framework for robust business growth. Business growth leads to customer growth and profitability.

In closing, let's look at the stragile manager, the stragile organization, customer relations, and stragile business management.

The Stragile Manager

Though it may seem daunting, changing the processes and mind-set of the individual manager is the single most critical step in the process. It requires an open mind and a willingness to adapt to a changing business environment.

As a stragile manager, you are responsible for growing and sustaining your business as well as identifying opportunities to grow by adapting to the changing market. Ultimately, it is by embracing and shaping change that the stragile manager can position himself or herself to deliver sustainable business growth.

The Stragile Organization

The stragile organization represents a change from a traditional vertical corporate hierarchy toward self-empowered individuals and teams. It's a focus on personal empowerment and developing engaged staff as a mechanism to drive improved customer outcomes. Empowerment may be difficult to define and measure, but the outcome is where employees have the responsibility and the authority to deliver to the customer's requirements.

Increased efficiencies and resulting business growth can be gained by simply letting your teams get on with their jobs. As a manager, you are responsible not for doing their jobs for them or micromanaging them but for governance, strategy, and facilitation. Being stragile means that you point your staff in the right direction and make sure there is nothing, whether internal or external, that will block their progress. You are not directly responsible for the completion of day-to-day tasks, but you are responsible for facilitating them. This distinction is important in stragile management because it is the responsibility of each individual employee to deliver on his or her day-to-day requirements.

An open and transparent organizational structure is key. One of the strengths of stragile management is the focus on staff engagement and developing staff as a mechanism to drive improved customer outcomes.

Customer Relations

Under stragile management, your teams and customers work closely together, collaborating toward the desired outcomes. Like the pro football quarterback, to be stragile means to be flexible and adaptable to changing circumstances, and nothing changes more than your customers' needs and desires. While it may be the hardest change to make, integrated customer engagement is an extremely effective part of a stragile management approach. It's about embedding your customers within the delivery processes, thereby ensuring they share in the accountability and responsibility for product delivery. By promoting these client partnerships, your organization will improve overall outcomes for your customers.

Stragile Business Management

By utilizing just-in-time planning and design and an incremental or continuous delivery process, stragile management allows for rapid change when scope and circumstances change. In an iterative or incremental work process that allows for rapid change when scope and circumstances change, customers can work alongside the team to shape and direct the outcomes, while (whenever possible) the team regularly delivers partial, though functional, products to the customer. The product itself continues to evolve as each iteration builds upon the last.

Becoming stragile is about change—changing how you think, changing how you work, and changing the way you interact. By accepting, embracing, and shaping change, you can take advantage of new opportunities and outperform and outcompete in the market.

While it sounds simple, change, by its very nature, is not easy. Stragile management is not a quick win, and it's not a three-step plan to a better business. Stragile management is hard work and requires a new way of thinking about the traditional business practices of hierarchical corporate structures, customer engagement, staff management, and work processes.

The technology of becoming stragile means the new ways we can sift the massive amounts of data to actually take action (via AI) and support the scientists and artists who run an organization.

The science is knowing what to look at and making sure you are delivering the solutions that fit the goals.

The art is all about getting the right strategy, aligning, and inspiring people (it goes without saying you have hired the right talent to do this—remember, hire slow and fire fast).

The road to becoming stragile is not necessarily easy, but you'll never know until you start. Remember—the deadly iceberg is lurking in the dark water somewhere ahead. You need to make sure that you see it and steer around it with plenty of room to spare. You want your passengers to arrive at their destination without a worry in the world, so that they'll have a great memory of your service and will never consider patronizing a competitor.

Strategy + agile = Stragile. It's a formula for success.